What I Did in the Holidays

A Play

Philip Osment

A SAMUEL FRENCH ACTING EDITION

SAMUEL FRENCH

FOUNDED 1830

SAMUELFRENCH-LONDON.CO.UK
SAMUELFRENCH.COM

WHAT I DID IN THE HOLIDAYS is fully protected under the copyright laws of the British Commonwealth, including Canada, the United States of America, and all other countries of the Copyright Union. All rights, including professional and amateur stage productions, recitation, lecturing, public reading, motion picture, radio broadcasting, television and the rights of translation into foreign languages are strictly reserved.

ISBN 978-0-573-01739-1

www.samuelfrench-london.co.uk

www.samuelfrench.com

FOR AMATEUR PRODUCTION ENQUIRIES

UNITED KINGDOM AND WORLD
EXCLUDING NORTH AMERICA
plays@SamuelFrench-London.co.uk
020 7255 4302/01

Each title is subject to availability from Samuel French,

depending upon country of performance.

What I Did In The Holidays

First presented by the Wolsey Theatre, Ipswich, in association with Cambridge Theatre on March 2nd, 1995 at The Wolsey Theatre, Ipswich, with the following cast of characters:

Eileen	Kate Byers
George	Chris Crooks
Frank	James Kerr
Cathy	Penny Layden
Robert	Steve Nicolson
Andy	Fergus O'Donnell
Morley	Anthony Taylor
Peggy	Jacqueline Tong

Directed by **Mike Alfreds**
Set, costumes and lighting designed by **Paul Dart**
Assistant Director **Robert Hale**

The play takes place over the school holidays of 1963

CHARACTERS

Morley, 11
Eileen, Morley's sister, 25
Frank, Morley's half brother, 19
Robert, Morley's brother, 21
George, their father, 60s
Catherine, a visitor from Glasgow, 20
Andy, a visitor from Glasgow, 17
Peggy, George's wife, mid/late 40s

SYNOPSIS OF SCENES

SCENE 1   Late July

SCENE 2   Early August

SCENE 3   Late August

SCENE 4   Late August

SCENE 5   Early September

SCENE 6   Early September

The play is set on a farm in Devon

Time: the summer of 1963

ACKNOWLEDGEMENT

What I Did in the Holidays was commissioned in 1993 and was developed in consultation with Mike Alfreds. I would like to thank all friends and colleagues who read the play at various stages, most particularly Noël Greig, Lin Coghlan, Jenny Topper, and Willie Elliott, who was my Scottish consultant. Special thanks to Nina Ward who read the play and discussed it with me at every stage.

Philip Osment

Also by Philip Osment, published by Samuel French:

The Dearly Beloved

WHAT I DID IN THE HOLIDAYS

SCENE 1

The farmhouse. A living room with a kitchen off it

It is raining

Kathleen Ferrier is singing "Blow the Wind Southerly" on the radio

Eileen and Morley are looking out the window

Morley They've been out there for ages.
Eileen They must be getting soaked.
Morley No-one will give them a lift.

Pause. They watch

Eileen Awful weather for hitchhiking.
Morley They must be on their holidays.
Eileen Mmmm.

Pause

Morley Where do you think they're from?
Eileen I don't know. (*She switches the radio off and moves to fill the Aladdin lamp with oil*)
Morley They might be from London.
Eileen Mmm.
Morley Or Bristol.
Eileen Hold this.

Morley holds the funnel

Morley Or Birmingham.

Eileen Mmmm.

Morley Or Blackpool.

Eileen Hold it still.

Morley Or Bath.

Eileen Morley!

Morley MMMMorley. Or Morecambe. Or Morchard Bishop.

Eileen Stop it.

Morley Or Moretonhampstead.

Eileen Is that it?

Morley Bit more. Mum always fills it right up. Or Minehead. Or Manchester.

Eileen Shut up, Morley.

Morley That's it.

Eileen Where's the top?

Morley Here. Or the Isle of Man. Or Moscow.

Eileen Give me the matches.

Morley Or Mexico. Or Outer Mongolia.

Eileen If you don't stop, I'll smack you. Give them to me.

Morley I'll do it.

Eileen You know what Mum says about you playing with matches.

Morley She's not here, though, is she?

Eileen lights the wick and they watch the flame creep round the wick

  Or the moon. Or Mars.

Eileen You miss her?

Morley Or Mercury. Or The Milky Way.

Eileen You're driving me mad, Morley. Be quiet.

Morley You're driving me mad, Morley. Be quiet.

Eileen Stop it.

Morley Stop it.

Eileen If you don't stop——

Morley If you don't stop——

Eileen What did you do today?

Morley What did you do today?

Eileen Morley!

Morley Morley!

They look at the lamp. Eileen hums "Blow the Wind Southerly". Morley imitates her

Eileen That's Mum's favourite song.

Morley stops humming and looks out of the window

Morley We never go anywhere.
Eileen Tell me what you did today.
Morley Didn't do anything.
Eileen First day of your holiday.
Morley Read my book.
Eileen You could have gone upover and helped Dad and Rob look for the spring for the new well.
Morley That's boring. Perhaps they're on an adventure.
Eileen Who?
Morley The hitchers.
Eileen Come here. (*She turns up the light*)

He goes to her and she starts pinning up the hem of his trousers

Morley Why are you doing this now?
Eileen I want to see if they're going to fit.
Morley It's ages before I start.
Eileen Surprising how quickly September will come.
Morley When you used to read *Famous Five*, did it make you sad?
Eileen No. Why should it?
Morley 'Cause they're friends.
Eileen Why does that make you sad?
Morley 'Cause they're all together.
Eileen Yes.
Morley And even if they quarrel they like each other really.
Eileen Mmmm.
Morley Do you think I'll make friends at grammar school?
Eileen Of course you will.
Morley David Buckingham's mum is buying him long trousers.
Eileen You don't need long trousers.
Morley These were Rob's.
Eileen They're all we can afford.
Morley Mum would let me have long ones.
Eileen We haven't got the money, Morley.
Morley We haven't got the money, Morley.

She jabs him with the pin

Aowwhhh.
Eileen Sorry.
Morley You're not.

She laughs

You did it on purpose.
Eileen I hardly touched you. (*She turns up the light*) Can't see properly.
Morley The electric never works.
Eileen Perhaps Frank will let us have some of his diesel.
Morley 'Nother leak!
Eileen Where?
Morley There.
Eileen My clean floor.

She runs out

Morley holds his hand out to the drip

Eileen enters with a saucepan

Morley There's a drip in my bedroom too. I had to put Dad's pot under it.
Eileen That'll mean another damp patch on your ceiling.
Morley Dad should have done the roof properly.

They look at the ceiling

Mum wouldn't have gone away if he did things properly.

She looks at him

Eileen You want a treat?
Morley What?

She gets a box of chocolates

Wow!

Eileen Just one, mind.
Morley Where did they come from?

She takes the wrapping off the chocolates

   Elly!
Eileen What?
Morley Where did you get them?
Eileen They were a present.
Morley Did Derek Rudd give them to you?

They look in the box

Eileen Strawberry cream. That's your favourite.

He takes the chocolate

Morley You've gone red.
Eileen I haven't.
Morley You have.

They eat their chocolate

   Are you going to marry Derek Rudd?

She does not respond

   Are you?
Eileen Course not.
Morley What's sex appeal?
Eileen Where did you hear that?
Morley Rob said to Dad that Derek Rudd hasn't got any.
Eileen You shouldn't eavesdrop.
Morley What's eavesdrop?
Eileen Listening to things you shouldn't.
Morley Have you got sex appeal?

Pause

Eileen Morley?

Morley What?
Eileen Don't say anything about these.
Morley Why not?
Eileen I don't want everyone going on about it.
Morley Can I have another?
Eileen Promise?
Morley Yes.

She lets him choose another chocolate and then hides the box

   I don't want you to marry Derek Rudd.
Eileen Mum will come back, Morley. She always comes back in the end.
Morley I know. Don't go on about it.

Eileen returns to pinning up the trousers

   Frank enters singing. He is carrying a bucket of milk

Frank   "We're going where the sun shines brightly,
                         We're going where the sea is blue.
                         You've seen it in the movies
                         Now let's see if it's true oooo."
Eileen You're late, Frank.
Frank (*singing*)   "Everybody has a summer holiday
                         Doing things they always wanted to..." (*He takes
                              off his boots and wet clothes*)
Eileen Where are Dad and Rob?
Frank Still upover looking for this spring.
Eileen They shouldn't be out in this.
Frank I've been out in it. No 'lectric?
Eileen There's no diesel for the generator.
Frank Told him we were getting low.
                         (*singing*) "Fun and laughter on our summer
                              holiday
                         For me and you ooo ooo."
   Had to get the cows across the road on my own. And feed Rob's pigs.
   Not doing that every night.
                         (*singing*) "For a week or two."

   Frank goes into the kitchen

Eileen Supper's nearly ready.
Frank (*off*) I'm having supper at Rosemary's.

Frank enters with a jug and some muslin

Had to get them two hitchhikers to stop the cars while I got the cows
across.
                                   (*Singing*) "We're going where the sun shines
                                       brightly." (*He sets up the jug with the muslin
                                       over it*)
Morley Where they from?
Frank Dunno. Sounded Irish.
Morley Irish?
Eileen Give Dad and Rob a shout.

Frank goes to the window

Frank Daaad! Daaaaaaad!
Eileen No need to make it sound like there's been a murder!

Morley giggles

Frank Rohhhhb!

They listen

Eileen They hear you?
Frank Dunno. Rohhhhhhb! (*To the hitchhikers*) Just calling my dad into
  supper. No luck yet, then?
Morley Where are they trying to get to?
Frank Ilfracombe. Daaaaaaaaaaaaaaaad.
Eileen They must have heard you.

Frank starts pouring the milk through the muslin into the jug

Frank (*singing*)   "We're all going on a summer holiday
                              Doing things we always wanted to
                              Everybody has a summer holiday..."
Eileen Frank?

Frank What?

Eileen Can't we use some of your diesel?

Frank I need it for the milking machine.

Eileen I just thought——

Frank You know what thought thought. He thought if you stuck a feather in the ground a hen would grow.

Pause

He's always doing this.

Eileen All right.

Frank And he never gives me the money for it. Why didn't he send Rob up for some.

Eileen Mandy works on the pumps.

Frank So just because Rob's fallen out with his girlfriend I have to suffer.

Pause

I don't see why I should have to supply the diesel for the generator. I'm trying to save. Let Rob pay for it.

Eileen Rob hasn't got any money.

Frank He's always got enough money to buy petrol for that car of his. It's all right for you. You've got your job at the library. You get a wage packet every week. I'm fed up with it. I'm just a bloody dogsbody round here.

Morley Don't get aereated.

Frank I was in a good mood till I come in here. S'pose there's no water for me to wash either.

Morley You going out?

Eileen You'll have to go down and get some.

Morley Going pictures?

Frank Mind your own business.

Morley Can I come?

Frank No, you bloody can't.

Morley He's going to sit in the back row snogging with Rosemary.

Eileen What's on?

Morley New Elvis film. Will you take me?

Eileen Maybe.

Morley Tonight?

Eileen I'm going out tonight.
Morley Who with? Derek Rudd?
Eileen Shut up, Morley.
Morley Nobody takes me anywhere.

Robert enters

Eileen Rob, you're soaking.

She goes to get him a towel. He takes off his boots and wet clothes

Frank Get Rob to take you to the pictures. He hasn't got anybody to go with.

Frank goes into the kitchen. He sings "Take These Chains From My Heart" off stage

Morley Will you?
Eileen You find a spring?
Robert In the end.
Eileen What's wrong?
Robert Nothing.
Morley Rob!
Robert What?
Morley Will you take me to the pictures?

Frank enters with a pail

Frank The ceiling's leaking in the kitchen.
Eileen I've just washed the floor.
Frank I put the milk bucket underneath.

Frank exits. He sings "Take These Chains From My Heart" off stage

Eileen Honestly.
Robert What?
Eileen I get home from work. There's no electricity. No water. The roof's leaking and Morley's getting on my nerves.
Morley I haven't done anything.

Robert You sound like Mum.

Eileen holds out Morley's farm trousers

Eileen Here, Morley.

Morley takes off the pinned-up trousers and puts on his farm trousers

Robert Those my old school trousers?
Eileen I'm altering them for Morley. (*She takes the school trousers and starts tacking them up*)
Robert Hated going to that school.
Morley You didn't go to grammar school.
Eileen Where's Dad?
Morley You went secondary modern.
Robert Talking to Mr Buckingham. He was over the other side of the stream watching us dig the well. He said to Dad, "You want go get a mechanical digger, George". Dad patted me on the back and said, "This is my mechanical digger". (*He laughs*) Henry Buckingham stood there laughing. He's back from Agricultural College.
Eileen I know.
Robert Oh yeah?
Eileen Someone said in the library.
Robert Thing about Henry Buckingham is he thinks he's the cat's whiskers because he's been away to college. Pathetic, isn't it? That's the height of achievement round here. People round here got no imagination. Stick-in-the-muds all of 'em. And they laugh at anybody who wants to be a bit different. They go round in their old bangers that they've had for ten years covered in hen's mess and cow shit and they think you're a bloody good-for-nothing just 'cause you've got a car with a bit of oomph about it. Makes me sick. He said to me, "I see you got a new car, then, Robert. Bit fast for our roads". I told him I might take a trip up to London in it. "What ee want to go to London for?" Typical. No ambition, see. Asked me if I was going to help organise the Young Farmers Club fancy dress. Bloody Young Farmers Club! All they do is sit around talking about the butter content of their milk. Bloody plodders. Wouldn't want to be like them.
Morley Henry Buckingham went to grammar school.
Eileen You going out tonight?

Robert Dunno.

Morley You could take me to the pictures, then.

Robert Fancy a ride into town later?

Morley She's going out with her boyfriend.

Robert He's another plodder. (*In a high squeaky voice*) I spend six days shearing sheep and on the seventh day I go preaching in the chapel.

Morley He gave her some chocolates. Look.

Eileen Morley!

Robert Oooohhh. He'll want a kiss tonight, then. Bet he's got a slobbery kiss.

Morley Ugghhhh.

Eileen Least he hasn't got engaged to somebody else.

Morley makes kissing noises

(*She slaps him hard*) Stop that.

Morley Aowwwhhh.

Eileen You're a little tell-tale.

Morley And you're a ratty ratface. I hate you.

Robert Don't be a baby.

Morley I'm telling Mum.

Robert Fat lot she cares.

Morley Shut up!

Pause

Robert Who told you?

Eileen 'Bout Mandy and Henry Buckingham?

Robert Yeah.

Eileen Everyone knows.

George enters

Take your boots off, Dad. I washed the floor tonight.

George Why haven't you got the lights on?

Robert No diesel.

George Use some of Frank's.

Morley He won't let us have any.

Eileen Says he hasn't got enough.

George Frank!

Frank enters. He has been washing

We want some of your diesel.

Frank Haven't got any.

George Only want a little bit for tonight.

Frank That's what you always say. I need it for tomorrow morning.

George You can go up the garage first thing.

Frank They don't open early enough.

George Hour or so either way won't hurt.

Frank I'll miss the milk lorry.

Robert You know he doesn't like his little routine upset, Dad.

Eileen The lamp's lit now.

Robert Creature of habit, our Frank. Just like his cows.

Frank ignores Robert and exits

George Go and get some, Rob.

Frank enters

Frank You can't have it.

Robert Don't be such a miser. Little bit of diesel either way isn't going
   to make any difference to you.

Frank (*to George*) Give me the money for it, then.

George Now look, who do those cows belong to?

Frank I have to milk them.

George And whose grass do they eat?

Frank And who buys the cake for them?

Robert You're so petty, Frank.

Frank (*looking at Robert for the first time with surprising intensity*) Shut
   up! Just shut up!

George There's that temper again. We know where that comes from.

Eileen Dad!

Frank exits

George That's Jerry temper. (*He fetches a petrol can and a piece of hose*)

Eileen You shouldn't say things like that.
George Here, Rob.
Eileen We can manage with the lamp.
Robert He'll only fly off the handle, Dad.
George Go and siphon off a bit of diesel.
Eileen Don't, Rob.

Robert puts on his boots and exits

George That little runt, Manfred, had a temper like that. He was a vicious
little bugger.
Eileen Shhhh.

Frank enters and puts on his boots

Frank Where's he going with that can?
Morley He's gone to get some of your diesel.

Frank exits after Robert

Eileen Morley!

Morley exits after Frank

You shouldn't go on about Frank's father in front of Morley.
George You heard from your mother?
Eileen Not since last week.
George Saw Buckingham upover.
Eileen Rob said.
George He's got a pump he doesn't need.
Eileen He's given Henry a partnership.
George Who told you that?
Eileen Mandy's mother came in the library. That's how Mandy and Henry
can get engaged.
George Did your mother say when she was coming back?
Eileen No.
George She'll be back.
Eileen Mmmmm.
George Once we get this water connected.

Eileen She'll say she wants mains water. You know what she's like.

George Shouldn't have to pay for your water. Falls from heaven. Should be free.

Eileen Mmmm.

George Soon have water on tap. Get the health inspector to pass it. Then you can write and tell her.

Eileen Lot of work.

George We'll find a way.

Eileen Rob's upset.

George What about?

Eileen Mandy.

George He'll get over it.

Eileen Mmmm.

George He wants thirty bob for it.

Eileen What?

George Buckingham. For the pump. Thought I'd go up and get it tonight.

Eileen You shouldn't have kept Rob away from school so much.

George I could teach him all he needs to know.

Eileen He's got an inferiority complex about it.

George You got any money?

Eileen Bit.

George Selling a calf tomorrow.

Eileen gets some money from her purse and gives it to him

Eileen He hasn't got anybody to go out with tonight.

Morley runs in

Morley Rob's hit Frank. Frank took the can off Rob and so Rob hit him with the pipe.

Frank enters. He is nearly in tears

Frank I'm fed up with it. It's not bloody fair.

Morley Frank's lost his temper.

Robert enters

Frank You keep away from me.

Robert I'm not going to touch you. Making such a fuss.
Frank You bloody hit me.
Robert I just tapped you.
Frank Bloody bully.
Morley You shouldn't bloody swear you bloody bugger.
Eileen Shut up, Morley.
George Give me back the can.

Robert tries to get the can from Frank. They struggle

Eileen Stop it! Stop it! Look at the mess you're making.

They stop

   You're driving me mad. All of you. I've had enough of it.

   Frank exits

Robert I hardly touched him.
Eileen You don't know your own strength.

   Eileen exits

Morley You're a bully. Bobby's a bully.
Robert It's your bedtime.
Morley It's holiday. Ha ha ha.
George She'll get over it.

   Frank enters and looks for his keys

Frank Who's had the keys for my scooter? (*To Morley*) Have you been
   playing with them?
Morley No.
Frank You sure?
Morley Yes.

Frank looks at Robert

Robert I haven't had them. Wouldn't be seen dead on your scooter.

Frank Someone's moved them. I'm going to be late.
George She'll have to wait.

Morley whispers in George's ear

  Go on, then.
Frank Give 'em back, Morley.

Morley goes to get the keys

George You give us some diesel first.

Morley gives the keys to George

Frank You're a troublemaker. You know that?
Morley And you're a liar.
Frank What you mean?
Morley You've got a whole can of diesel hidden in the loft.
Frank You want to keep your nose out of things. Might get it chopped off.

Frank grabs hold of Morley's nose

Morley Aowwwhhh.

  Eileen enters with plates and cutlery

George Leave him.
Frank You little bugger.

Frank hits Morley

Morley You're not my real brother.
Eileen Morley.
Morley You're a Jerry.

Pause

George (*giving Frank the keys*) Now, son, go and put that diesel in the
  generator.

Frank I'm glad I'm only your half brother. Maybe I won't turn out like the rest of you. Look at him, he's a laughing stock driving around in his Riley. Can't even keep a girlfriend.

George Go on. Let's get these lights on.

Frank exits

Eileen You're never to say things like that.

Morley What?

Robert I hardly touched him, Elly.

Pause

Want some help?

Eileen It's OK.

Robert When's Derek picking you up?

Eileen I said I'd ring him from the phone box.

Morley Dad?

George What?

Morley Will you take me to the pictures?

George Dunno, boy.

Robert I'll do the washing up tonight.

Morley Please, Dad.

George Maybe next week.

Morley The Elvis film won't be on next week.

Eileen (*to Robert*) Aren't you going town?

Robert No.

Eileen I'll go with you.

Robert Thought you had a date.

Eileen Oh that... (*She laughs*)

Robert All right, then.

Morley I want to go.

Robert You can't.

Morley I want to see the film. Dad!

George Quiet, boy.

Morley I want to see it. It's Elvis. (*He cries*)

Frank enters

Frank Those hitchers want to know if they can camp.

George Tell 'em to come in.

Frank exits

Eileen follows him out

Robert You going to let 'em?
George Why not?
Robert Don't put them in the field with the bull.
George He could go upover.
Robert He'll get out on the road if you do that.

Eileen enters with Andy and Catherine. Andy is wearing a cowboy hat

Catherine Hope we're no bothering you.
George You look a bit wet.
Catherine Ay we're soakin'.

Andy takes off his haversack

　　OK?
Andy Yeah.
Robert Come far, have you?
Catherine From Bristol the day. Cosy here, i'n't it? Look at that lamp.
　　I've never seen a lamp like that.
George Hitched all the way?
Catherine Ay.
Eileen On holiday?
Catherine ⎫　　　　　⎧ No exactly.
Andy　　 ⎭ *(together)* ⎩ Yeah.
Catherine My aunty used tae work in a hotel down here every summer.
　　She always used tae say how nice it was here. So we thought we might
　　get a job down here.
George Ahhh. You hungry?
Catherine A bit.
George Spec' we've got enough to go round, haven't we, Elly?
Eileen Think so.
Catherine Thank you.
Eileen You're from Scotland.

Catherine Ay, Glasgow.
George What sort of work you looking for?
Catherine Anything, really. (*She starts to take her coat off*)
Eileen Robert!

Robert helps Catherine take her coat off

This is my brother Robert.
Catherine I'm Catherine.
Robert Hallo.
Catherine Hi.
Eileen I'm Eileen, and this is our Dad.
Catherine How d'ye do.

Catherine shakes their hands. She sees Morley, who is still tearful

And who are you?
Eileen That's Morley.
George My youngest.
Catherine How d'ye do.
Morley (*mimicking her*) How d'ye do?

Laughter

Catherine This is Andy.
Morley Andy Stewart!

More laughter

Is he your boyfriend?
Catherine No.
Eileen Your brother?
Andy No.
Catherine My friend's brother. Wilma. She was going to come with us
    but she couldnae in the end. So we came anyway.
Eileen All the way from Scotland.
Morley I can sing "The Scottish Soldier". Do you know it?
Andy Ay.
Morley Ay.

Eileen Morley!
Andy What are those birds?
Eileen Pardon?
Andy The birds under your roof.
Robert The what?
Eileen Buds? On the roses?
Catherine The birds. They've wee nests along under the slates on your
    byre.
Robert They're house-martins.
Eileen They come every summer.
Catherine It's lovely here. I cannae get over that lamp.

There is the sound of an engine starting up

George Turn the switch, Morley.

*Morley does so. Slowly, a flickering light comes on, which gradually gets
brighter and steadier. All the family respond with pleasure; Catherine
with disappointment*

    That's better.

SCENE 2

A field

Morley enters with Catherine

She stands looking

Morley That's the moor over there.
Catherine Ay. Eileen took me up there last week. It's beautiful.
Morley See that farm over there?
Catherine Yes.
Morley That belonged to Mr Kingdom.
Catherine It's right up on the moor. Must be great to live up there.
Morley He hanged himself in his barn.
Catherine Oh dear.

Morley Yeah. He shot his wife with a shotgun first.

Catherine Why did he do that?

Morley He was depressed. His face was blue when they found him. And that's Mr Buckingham's farm.

Catherine Ah-ha.

Morley His fields are greener than ours. That's because he's a proper farmer.

Catherine Yes?

Morley Mum says Dad isn't a proper farmer.

Catherine I see. There's Andy in the well. Hallo! I've brought your dinner.

Morley Hallo! Frank! Rob! Cathy's brought your dinner.

Catherine Andy! Come and have your piece.

Morley Your what?

Catherine Piece. Do you not know what that is?

Morley No.

Catherine It's what my dad always took to work with him. A cheese piece.

Morley A sandwich!

Catherine OK. A sandwich. (*Shouting*) Will I bring it down to you?

Morley What did he say?

Catherine Don't bother.

Morley Don't bother wi' me piece!

She laughs

They're going to get the pump working today.

Catherine Why do they no just put the pump on the well in the orchard?

Morley 'Cause the man from the council said that water might have germs in it. It's too near the buildings and all the pig's mess and cow's mess can just run into it.

Catherine Ughhh.

Morley That's why we have to boil all the water. Mum was doing cream teas but they closed us down. They said it wasn't hygienic. See that shed over there? That's my museum.

Catherine Your museum?

Morley It's where I keep my collection. Do you want to see it?

Catherine Ay. When I've had a wee rest.

Morley Shall we lie in the grass?

They lie in the grass

Sometimes I lie in the grass and pretend that I'm on the run and I've got
to hide. And if Dad or Rob or anyone sees me, then I'll get caught.

Catherine All on your own?

Morley Yes.

Catherine Are there no other wee boys around here?

Morley Only David Buckingham. I don't like him. Shall we play that?

Catherine OK. Why don't you like him?

Morley He made me put my hand in a cow-pat. There's Rob.

Catherine That looks heavy.

Morley It's a rock. They must have dug it up.

Catherine It's huge.

Morley Rob's really strong. He's stronger than anyone.

Catherine Is he?

Morley Yes. He can lift four bales at the same time.

Catherine Really?

Morley He stopped a fight at a dance once by knocking the blokes' heads
together.

Catherine Did he?

Morley Yeah. Do you like his car?

Catherine Ay.

Morley Dad got it him for his twenty-first birthday from the car auction.
Eileen paid for some of it though. He went a hundred and seven in it on
the dual carriageway.

Catherine Really?

Morley Have you ever been that fast?

Catherine Not in my boss's wee car. He had a fit if I went over thirty.

Morley Can you drive?

Catherine Ay.

Morley Why were you driving your boss's car?

Catherine He taught me.

Pause

Morley Rob goes courting in the Riley.

Catherine Does he?

Morley Yes.

Catherine Has he got a lot of girlfriends?

Morley Quite a few. His last one was called Mandy. He's doing a wee wee. Look.

Catherine looks away

   Rob!
Catherine Don't.
Morley You can't see anything. He's got his back to us.

She hides

   He's gone.
Catherine What happened to Mandy?
Morley Her father didn't like her going out with Rob because Dad sold him a sow that always eats her piglets.
Catherine (*jumping*) Ughhhh.
Morley What?
Catherine A wee beastie.

Morley laughs

   I don't like creepy crawly things.

They lie in the grass

Morley What was your job?
Catherine Eh?
Morley In Scotland.
Catherine I was a waitress. In an Italian restaurant.
Morley Didn't you like it?
Catherine It was OK.
Morley So why did you come down here?
Catherine I fancied a change.

Andy creeps up behind them and jumps on Catherine. He is covered in mud

Andy Aaaaarghhhh.
Catherine Och. Don't. You gave me such a fright. Stop it.

Andy (*putting mud on her and singing*) Three wee craws,
                         Sittin' on a wa', sittin' on a wa', sittin' on a wa',
                         Sittin' on a wa' aw aw aw.
Catherine Stop it, Andy.

Andy lies on top of her

Andy   Three wee craws sittin' on a wa'
                                On a cold and frosty morning.

They stop and look at each other

Can you feel it? Feel it.
Catherine Don't.

They look at Morley. Andy goes to put mud on him

   Morley runs away

You've scared him.
Andy He's a wee jessie, that one.
Catherine Leave him. It's OK, Morley. He willnae touch you.
Andy I'm famished.
Catherine Are yees nearly finished?
Andy There's a root of a tree in the way.
Catherine Here.

She gives him a sandwich. He eats

Andy That root's really thick. I tried tae pull it out with my hands. But it
   goes right down intae the earth. Frank says it probably comes from that
   tree way over there. You'd never believe the roots would go that far. It's
   amazing, i'n't it?
Catherine I went to the phone box this morning. Phoned Wilma at her
   work.
Andy And?
Catherine The naval whatchamecallems had been to the house.
Andy The reggies.
Catherine Them.

Andy I'm no going back.
Catherine OK.
Andy Ye didnae tell Wilma where we are?
Catherine She willnae tell.
Andy Did ye?
Catherine No.
Andy She's a big gob.

Pause

Did you phone the restaurant and speak to Mr Capaldi as well?
Catherine Course not.
Andy Thought mebbe you'd be missing your sugar daddy.
Catherine Don't be stup't.
Andy Does he know where you are?
Catherine I didnae even tell him I was leaving.

Morley enters

Andy (*splattering him with mud and singing*) The first wee craw was
                              greetin' for his maw
                         Greetin' for his maw.
                         Greetin' for his maw aw aw aw.
Catherine Don't. It's OK, Morley. I'll wipe it off.

She wipes Morley with her hanky. Andy picks his nose

Andy Oh, look, a great big snotter. Look, Morley.
Catherine Will ye stop that, Andy!

Andy chases him. Morley runs away. Andy pretends to rub it in on Morley

Stop it.

Andy leaves Morley

What's wrong wi' you?
Andy Nothing.
Catherine You're forever bullying that wee boy.
Andy Do ye no like it, Morley?

Morley does not answer

Your Aunty Catherine will kiss it better.

Catherine Ye want tae grow up. You get so jealous, you. He's just a wee
   boy.

Andy Well, we all know about you and wee boys.

Pause

I waited for ye last night.

Catherine I couldnae, Andy. They'd hear us.

Andy I thought maybe you and Morley.

Catherine Shut it.

Catherine hits Andy. Morley watches

   Eileen enters

Eileen Thought you'd all be up here.

Catherine You no at work the day, Eileen?

Eileen Library closes midday on a Wednesday.

Catherine Forgot.

Eileen They finished?

Catherine There's a wee problem with the root of a tree. I didnae bring
   you any dinner.

Eileen I've had some. (*She sits with Catherine*)

   Andy wanders off

Catherine I put clean sheets on the bed the day.

Eileen Thanks. You all right in Mum's room?

Catherine It's great. You sure it's OK?

Eileen I wished you'd said something sooner.

Catherine Och, it was fine.

Eileen It wasn't until you asked about sleeping in the barn that it even
   occurred to me. I feel awful. You been out there two weeks now.

Catherine I feel awful that Andy's taken Morley's room.

Eileen Morley's often had to share with Frank and Rob. Better than you
   having to share that tent with Andy.

Catherine Ay.
Eileen (*quietly*) He seems a bit young.
Catherine Andy?
Eileen Yes.
Catherine I'm used tae sharing. I was forever having tae share at home.
Eileen Big family?
Catherine Yes.
Eileen I always wanted to be Roman Catholic. It looks more ... well ...
    religious. Everyone's Methodist around here. (*In a very broad accent*)
    Us all goes to chapel!
Catherine A funny bloke called in the day.
Eileen Who?
Catherine I couldnae understand him. Speaks in dialect. Got a really high
    squeaky voice.
Eileen Blue car?
Catherine Ay. He left a letter for you.
Eileen I got it. It was my invitation to the Young Farmers Club Fancy
    Dress Ball at the end of August.
Catherine That's Derek?
Eileen Yes.

Pause

Catherine A lot of the farmers round here I cannae understand.
Eileen No.
Catherine He seemed very nice.
Eileen If a boy takes you out and tries to be too nice I don't like it.
Catherine It's no a problem I've had to deal wi'.
Eileen It just makes me nasty. I end up saying something really spiteful.
    I told him he was too plodding the other day.
Catherine What did he say?
Eileen Nothing. Just sat there.
Catherine (*laughing*) Oh dear.
Eileen He said, "I try, Eileen. I try". (*She laughs*) I wanted to slap him.

They start giggling

    He always comes round to open the car door for me. The other night I
    deliberately opened it myself and banged his shin.

They roll around laughing

Catherine You're crazy, Eileen. I've never met anyone like you.
Eileen He makes me want to say rude words. Like "piss" and "shit".

Catherine laughs

Morley Eileen!
Eileen Go away, Morley.

They laugh more

　You have many friends in Glasgow?
Catherine Some.
Eileen Who's Wilma?
Catherine She's my sister.
Eileen I thought you said she was Andy's sister.
Catherine Did I? No. She's my sister. She's no Andy's sister.
Eileen Always wanted a sister.

Pause

Catherine So are you going to go to the dance with Derek?
Eileen Don't know. Will you come?
Catherine Havenae been asked.
Eileen Mmmmm.

　Robert, Frank and George enter

Catherine Here's your piece.
Morley That means sandwich.
Robert Thank you.

They all take their sandwiches

Catherine I hear you found a tree root.
Frank Bloody great thing. Us needs a chain saw, Dad.
George Rob'll chop it out.
Morley Yesterday Rob chopped down a tree this big in eleven minutes.

Catherine Quite a man.

Eileen giggles

Morley I timed him.
Robert Frank didn't believe his eyes.
Frank Get off! Get off! Bloody wasp.
Robert He went down to get the saw. Time he came back I'd chopped the whole tree down. Hadn't I, Frank?
Frank Yeah. Get off.
Robert If you flap at it, it'll sting you. He said, "Yer, you'll rupture yourself if you're not careful". All right, Andy boy?
Andy Ay.
Robert Ay. He's a good little worker.

He squeezes Andy's arm

Got quite a muscle there.
Catherine He's been learning to box in the——
Robert What?
Andy In the Boys' Brigade.
Robert I'll give you a fight.
Morley Rob's muscle is really big.

The insect buzzes around Eileen. She screams

Robert Don't be daft. It's only a wasp. Come on, Andy.
Andy What?
Robert Let's see your muscle.

Eileen raises her eyebrows to Catherine. Catherine giggles

Morley Let's see yours, Rob.
Robert Mmmmm?
Morley Go on. Please.

Robert flexes his arm

Eileen (*to the insect*) Get off.

Robert For God's sake! She's a farmer's daughter too.
Eileen It looks bigger than a wasp.

Morley feels Rob's muscle

Morley Look.

Robert indicates his stomach

Robert Go on.

Morley punches him

  Solid as a rock.

Eileen screams and swats the insect

  It won't hurt you.
Eileen I don't like them.
Robert Don't be daft.
Eileen Shut up.
Robert You get hysterical.
Eileen Leave me alone.
Robert Temper, temper!
Frank There it is.

Catherine and Eileen both scream

Catherine I don't like them either, Eileen.
Andy Don't send it tae me.
Robert It won't sting you.
Frank Looks more like a hornet. Get off!

Morley hits Robert in the stomach when he is not expecting it

Robert Aowwhhh.
Morley What?
Robert What did you do that for?

The others smirk. Catherine giggles

George I want you to drive me into town this afternoon, Cathy.

Eileen Why you going town?

George I want to see the planning people. They say the well's gotta be further from the stream.

Eileen I told you.

George They'll be all right once I've talked to 'em.

Catherine I was going to wash the sheets.

George Eileen'll do that. Won't you, Elly?

Catherine It's her afternoon off.

George She'll be all right.

Catherine Can you no drive yourself?

Eileen He's lost his licence.

George Bloody policeman only stopped the car 'cause it was me.

Morley There's the hornet.

Eileen Where?

Eileen gets up and runs away

Morley It's on the back of your head, Cathy.

Catherine screams. Morley laughs

Catherine Where is it? Where is it? Get it off me. Andy!

Andy I'm no touching it.

Everyone except Catherine is laughing. She runs around with the insect chasing her. Morley laughs hysterically. Catherine is almost in tears with panic

Robert Let me get it. (*He goes towards Catherine and tries to swat the insect*)

Eileen Careful. It'll sting you.

Catherine Is it still there?

George It's gone.

There is a brief moment of waiting to see if the insect has gone. Catherine listens and watches. Suddenly she hears it

Catherine No, it isnae. (*She runs towards the others*)

They all run away from her because the insect is following her. More screams. Catherine trips over. Robert trips over her

Robert There it is. (*He swats it*) All right?
Catherine Where is it?
Robert It's gone. You OK?
Catherine Yes, thanks. I was stung by a bee once when I was little.
Robert Can be nasty. (*He smiles at Catherine*)

Andy watches Catherine's face. Eileen is looking at Robert and Catherine. They all sit again

Andy Anything to drink?
Catherine Here. (*She gets up to give him some lemonade*)
George Nice sandwich.
Robert Yeah.
Morley Eileen never puts enough butter on.
Robert She always scrapes it on. (*He smiles at Catherine*)
Eileen The postman's been, Morley. Brought you this card.

She gives him a postcard

Robert Who's it from?
Eileen Who do you think?
Robert Let's see.
Morley No. It's mine.
George From his mother?
Eileen She says she might come down at the end of the month.
Morley How do you know?
Eileen I read it.
Morley You shouldn't have. It's my card.
Catherine Is she on holiday?
Robert Something like that.
Eileen She's working in Hastings.

Robert takes the card

Morley Give it back.
Robert Nice picture of the pier.

Morley Tell him to give it back.

Robert teases Morley, keeping the postcard just out of his reach

Elly!
Robert Don't be such a baby
Eileen Give it back, Rob.
Morley You can't read it anyway. See if you can. He can't.
Robert (*reading*) "Dear Morley, how's my——"
Morley Told you he couldn': read it.
Eileen Rob.
Robert "How's my——"
Eileen "...darling..."
Robert "...darling boy?" Aaaahhhh. "Bill's going to drive me down to see you on the last..."
Eileen "...weekend in August."
Robert "...weekend in August. He wants to meet you." More fool Bill.

Eileen looks at George

"Hope you're being yourself."
Morley Being? It doesn't say that. Stupid.
Eileen "Behaving". You're not though, are you?
Robert "...behaving yourself. I'm missing you. Lots of love and kisses, Mum". Isn't that sweet? Are you missing your mummy too?
Morley Shut up; it was my card.
Robert Cry-baby.
Morley Shut up. Shut up'
Robert Here.
Morley I hate you. I hate all of you.

Morley runs off

Eileen Now look what you've done.
Robert She should be here looking after him.

Pause

It was only a bloody postcard.

Catherine Who's Bill?
Eileen The man she's housekeeping for.

Pause. Robert rests his arm on the ground and is stung

Robert Aowwh.
Eileen What?
Robert That bloody hornet. It was there. Aowwwhhh.
Frank Thought it was a wasp.

Catherine nudges Eileen, who starts to giggle

Robert It's not funny, Eileen.

*This makes Catherine and Eileen laugh more. The others join in. Robert
shakes his head at them in disdain*

Eileen (*laughing*) Let's have a look.
Robert (*angrily*) Get off.

*Pause. Robert sucks on his hand. Catherine tries not to giggle, hiding
behind Eileen. Frank and Andy are also trying to hide the fact that they are
laughing. Catherine snorts, which makes the others burst out laughing*

Eileen Do you want me to see if I can get it out?
Robert (*roughly*) No.
Eileen All right.
Robert Leave me alone.
Eileen Now you know what it feels like.
Robert Don't be so bloody pathetic. You've never been stung, anyway.

Pause

Catherine I should have some cream here. (*She looks in her bag and takes
out a tube*) Let's see.

Robert shows her his hand

   Does it hurt?
Robert No.

Catherine It's really swelling.

*Frank starts singing the chorus of "It's Now or Never" to himself,
unaware that what he is singing is apposite*

That better?
Robert Bit.

Frank is singing the first stanza of the song

Eileen Do you dance, Andy?
Andy Eh?
Eileen You could take Catherine to the Young Farmers Club Fancy Dress.
  Derek could easily get two more tickets. He's secretary.
Catherine He's two left feet when it comes tae ballroom dancing. He only
  knows the twist.
Robert I'll take you.
Catherine Oh.
Eileen Thought you weren't going.
Robert Never said that.
Eileen Andy might want to go.
Andy No.

Frank is singing the chorus again

Catherine You've a good voice, Frank.
Robert He likes Elvis.
Catherine I used to be a Cliff fan. I like John now, though. And Ringo.
Frank (*shocked*) You don't!
Catherine I went to see them.
Frank Live?
Catherine Ay.

Frank finds this hilarious

Frank Bloody hell! All that screaming!
Andy She likes Susan Maugham an all.

*Andy sings two lines from "Bobby's Girl". They ignore him. During the
following, he takes his shirt off and lies down, closing his eyes*

George Better get that pump going, Frank.
Frank Idn any petrol in it.
George Go up the garage on your scooter and get some.

George and Frank look at each other

You got a half crown, Rob?
Robert No.

George looks at Eileen

Eileen I haven't got my purse.
Catherine Hang on. (*She looks in her bag*) Here you are.

She passes some money to George, who gives it to Frank

Frank exits, singing the next stanza of the song

George She's doing a grand job, this girl.
Eileen Mmmm.
George Helped me feed the calves this morning. We'll make a proper
farmer of her.

Eileen starts picking up the remains of the food

Catherine Leave all that, Eileen.
Robert I haven't had a drink yet.
Eileen Hurry up, then.
Catherine I'll bring it down.
Robert Leave it, for God's sake. Stop fussing.
Eileen You're so bossy, you. I'm fed up with it. Think you can tell
everyone what to do. Maybe they don't want to do what you want them
to do.
Robert What's up with you?
Eileen There's nothing wrong with me. It's you. You want to learn a bit
of give and take. You're just a selfish pig.

Eileen exits

Robert What's got into her?

George She'll soon cool off.
Catherine I'll go and help her with the washing. Eileen! Wait for me.
George Need to be in town before the town hall closes.
Catherine We'll manage. Eileen!

She picks up the food and exits

George and Robert stand watching her

George Bloody good girl.
Robert Mmmm.
George Reminds me of Kate Ledger.
Robert The one you used to take out in her pony and trap?
George Lovely girl. Had hair just like that.
Robert Why didn't you marry her?
George Got TB.
Robert You never told me that.
George (*singing*) "I'll take you home again, Kathleen".
Robert So Mum's bringing this bloke.
George Soon get rid of that bugger.
Robert Yeah.
George End of the month, she say?
Robert Yeah.
George Should have the water laid on by then.
Robert Fancy bringing him with her.
George He'll get my foot up his backside.

Morley enters

Robert (*indicating Morley*) Little pigs!
George Better get into town.

George exits

Robert (*to Morley*) You're a selfish little bugger.

Morley pokes his tongue out at him. Robert kicks Andy

Wakey, wakey.

Andy (*with surprising ferocity*) You kick me again, pal, and you'll regret it.

Robert All right, all right.

Robert goes out, back to the well

Andy lies on his back, looking straight up at the sky

Morley I hate him. Do you?

Andy You see that cloud way up there?

Morley Which one?

Andy That one. It looks like a man on a horse.

Morley I can't see it. (*He lies down near Andy*)

Andy There. You see that wee bit sticking out?

Morley Yes.

Andy Well, just tae the top of that. That's the horse's head. He's got steam coming out of his nostrils. See it?

Morley Yeah.

Andy And there's the man on his back.

Morley Oh yeah, I can see it now.

Andy That's Matt Devine on his palomino stallion.

Morley Who's Matt Devine?

Andy Do ye no know Matt Devine? He's the fastest draw in the West.

Morley And what's his horse called?

Andy Ahh ... that's ... ahhh ... that's Cloud, of course.

Morley What, the horse is called Cloud?

Andy Ay, what else? Kepaow. Kepaow. The bad guys are in the rocks above Devil's Canyon when Matt rides through. Kepaow. Kepaow. He takes cover behind a boulder. Kepaow. (*In Matt's voice*) "Steady, Cloud." (*In Jake's voice*) "We're going to kill you, Matt Devine." (*In Matt's voice*) "That's what you think, Jake." Kepaow. Kepaow. (*In Jake's voice*) "Aaaaargghhhh. He got me." The bad guy falls down. Dead. (*In Matt's voice*) "You wanna feel a bullet in your chest too, Trampas?" (*In Trampas's voice*) "You won't get me, Devine!" Kepaow.

Morley giggles

(*In Matt's voice*) "You shot Cloud. That's it, Trampas!" Kepaow. Kepaow. Kepaow. Kepaow. (*In Matt's voice*) "Nobody hurts my horse, Trampas. You had to die."

Morley is entranced

Morley Was Cloud dead?
Andy No. Just hit in the leg. Matt Devine had to ride him into town to see the horse doctor. (*He makes the sound of a horse trotting lamely. He lies on the grass looking at the clouds again*)

Morley studies him

Morley You've got a spider on you. (*He reaches out and takes the spider on to his finger from Andy's arm. He looks at it on his finger. He blows it off. He points at Andy's side*) What's that?
Andy What?
Morley That scar.
Andy That's where Jake's bullet got me. (*He closes his eyes*) Mmmm. It's great. That sun.

Morley reaches out and touches the scar

    What are you doing?
Morley Nothing.

Pause

    Was it really a gunshot?
Andy Ay.
Morley Really?
Andy No.
Morley What was it?
Andy A knife.

Morley traces the scar

SCENE 3

The living room

Eileen is scrubbing the floor

Robert enters

Robert Just wanted to use the looking-glass.

Eileen Don't go where I've washed.

Robert Aren't you going to get changed?

Eileen Yes. After I've done this.

Robert Trust her to arrive just when we're all trying to get ready. (*He looks at himself in the mirror*) It's quite a good fit. Uncle Sonny's old tuxedo. You think I need a badge?

No response

    Elly!

Eileen A badge?

Robert O-o-seven.

Eileen Thought you had a gun.

Robert I can't wave that around all the time.

Eileen Mmmmmm.

Robert What's Cathy doing?

Eileen Making some scones for tea.

Morley runs in with a bunch of wild flowers

Morley I've picked these. I'm going to do an arrangement.

Eileen Careful.

Morley Where's that pretty vase?

Eileen Which one?

Morley Mum's favourite.

Eileen In the kitchen.

He runs towards the kitchen

    Don't make a mess. I've just cleaned up out there.

Morley All right, Ratty.

Morley exits

Robert Don't know why you bother. She'll still complain however clean it is. Has Dad emptied his chamber pot?

Eileen I don't know.

Robert You know how she went on about that the last time she came home.

Eileen They're only calling in, you know.
Robert Isn't she staying the night?
Eileen No. They're going down to Cornwall to see this Bill's mother.
Robert Does Morley know that?
Eileen I haven't said anything.
Robert What a mother

George enters

George Not here yet, then?
Eileen Don't get mud on this floor.
George Should be here by now.
Robert Get the tank filled up?
George Need more jubilee clips. You make much on the logs?
Robert Four quid or so.
George I want to get taps.
Robert I gave Cathy and Andy ten bob each.
George Just need a couple of quid.
Eileen Frank's on the warpath. Wants his wages.
Robert This arrived today from the solicitors.
George What is it?
Robert Tells you about how to draw up a partnership.
George Mmmm. Where's my black trousers, Elly?
Robert What you want them for?
George Wanted to put 'em on.
Robert I'm wearing them for my costume.
George Gave five bob for those.
Eileen Your suit trousers are clean.
George Need a clean shirt, too.
Eileen There's one in the chest of drawers on the landing.

George starts to go

Don't forget to wash your neck first.
Robert You want to look at this?
George Better have me wash.

George exits

Eileen Dad!

George (*off*) What?
Eileen Empty your pot.

She returns to her scrubbing

Robert Pathetic, really, isn't it?
Eileen What?
Robert Him getting all spruced up for her.
Eileen Mmmm.
Robert God! Fancy being married to a woman like that. (*He looks at the forms*) Looks fairly straightforward. What's that word?
Eileen Inheritance.
Robert Something about death duties. A partnership gets round that, you see.
Eileen I hate talking about things like that.
Robert Ought to get it sorted out. Sooner the better.
Eileen He's not going to die for years.

Morley enters with the flowers. He also has a very sharp knife

He puts the flowers in the middle of the table

Robert Very nice. Mummy will like them.

Morley starts to go

Eileen What you doing with that knife?
Morley Andy needs it.
Eileen What for?
Morley He caught a rabbit in that trap. He's going to skin it and we're going to make a camp-fire.
Eileen Don't get yourself dirty.

Morley exits

Robert First time I've known Morley interested in skinning a rabbit.
Eileen That's Andy's influence.
Robert 'Bout time he started doing things normal boys do.
Eileen They made a terrible mess in the bedroom. They've painted a cowboy on the wall. He's a funny boy, Andy.

Robert S'pose.

Eileen Don't really understand that relationship.

Robert What relationship?

Eileen Cathy and Andy.

Robert He used to be her boyfriend, that's all. Nothing funny about it. What are you going as, anyway?

Eileen Ruth.

Robert Ruth who?

Eileen Ruth from the Bible.

Robert Oh.

Eileen I've made one of those blue curtains into a long dress. And I'm going to wear that big white shawl over my head.

Robert You'll look more like the Virgin Mary.

Eileen I'm going to carry a basket with a sheaf of corn.

Robert Why?

Eileen Like I've been gleaning.

Robert Gleaning?

Eileen That's what she did.

Robert Did she?

Eileen Don't you remember Ruth and Naomi?

Robert Vaguely.

Eileen Naomi was her mother-in-law and when Ruth's husband died she stayed with her. (*She stops scrubbing*) "Whither thou goest, I will go; and where thou lodgest, I will lodge".

Robert Oh yeah.

Eileen Then they fell on hard times and she had to go out picking up corn in the fields. Gleaning. Gran had that picture of Ruth in the Alien Corn.

Robert Cathy's made herself a kilt.

Eileen I know.

Robert She was going to go as a geisha girl.

Eileen Mmmmm.

Robert Why don't you ask her if you can borrow her dressing-gown and go as that.

Eileen I'm going as Ruth.

Robert Please yourself.

Eileen You haven't even seen my costume and you're already criticising it.

Robert I'm not.

Pause

What's Derek going as?
Eileen Charlie Chaplin.

Robert laughs

Robert He's a good bloke.
Eileen Mmm.
Robert Reliable.
Eileen I suppose.
Robert Feel sorry for him, really.
Eileen Why?
Robert The way you treat him.
Eileen What do you mean, the way I treat him?
Robert He's obviously smitten.
Eileen So?
Robert You can't go through life looking for the perfect person, Elly.

Eileen does not respond

Cathy thinks Derek Rudd would be very good for you.
Eileen Does she?
Robert She says you need someone who'll look after you. Treat you like
a lady. She's a good judge of character. Shrewd, see? You should have
seen her buttering up old Hetherington-Smythe this afternoon. We went
up there to see if he wanted to buy some logs. He doesn't usually get any
in the summer. She told him how nice his garden was and admired his
lawn. Charmed him. Ended up buying half the load.
Eileen Excuse me.

He moves. She scrubs

Robert Thing about Cathy is her independence. How many girls would
be able to do what she did this summer? Just hitched to the other end of
the country. Takes a lot of courage to do that, you know. Didn't have
anything fixed up.
Eileen I went to Bristol on my course.
Robert You came home every weekend. Trouble with you, Elly, you're
too self-sacrificing. You don't want to get stuck here. I mean, look at
Aunty Pam. She lived for Dad and Uncle Sonny. Then when they got
married, she never got over it. You don't want to end up like her.

Catherine enters, wearing a kilt and carrying a plate of scones

Catherine There we are.
Robert A Scots girl in the Alien Corn, eh, Elly.
Catherine What?
Robert These look nice. (*He goes to take one*)

They struggle

Catherine Don't. They're for tea.

He eats a scone

Robert Mmmmm. Lovely.
Catherine You should wait.

They giggle

Will I put some jam in your sponge, Eileen?
Eileen I'll do that, thank you.

Eileen exits with the bucket of water

Robert I'll bloody kill her!
Catherine Don't.
Robert Going around with a face like a poker. It's not natural.
Catherine What?
Robert The way she behaves.

He kisses her

Catherine Careful.
Robert Come on.
Catherine I ought to get my make-up on.
Robert You don't need make-up. (*He moves to kiss her again*)
Catherine Shhh.

Eileen enters, crosses and exits

Robert and Catherine giggle

You havenae got your bow-tie on.
Robert It's upstairs.

She kisses him

Catherine Go on. (*She looks at herself in the glass for a long time. Then she starts putting her make-up on*)

Andy enters with the knife. He has blood all over his hands and face

He stands looking at her. She suddenly sees him and jumps

What have you done?
Andy Nothing. (*He finds a piece of string*)

She returns to her make-up. He looks at her and starts whistling "Bobby's Girl". He has a rabbit's foot which he binds with the string

Morley runs in

Morley Ugh. It was horrible. He took the rabbit's insides out. I'm going to put the rabbit's foot in my museum. I've got blood on my finger. Look.
Catherine Get away, Morley.
Morley Yeeughhhh.
Catherine Stop it!
Andy Brings you good luck, a rabbit's foot. You should wear it round your neck.
Morley Ughhh.
Catherine You're revolting.
Andy Look at that, all the wee strings in its legs. Look.

Morley draws away

It willnae hurt you. Look. Touch it.

Morley draws near

Take it.

Morley No.
Andy Blood. Blood. Go on.
Morley No.

Andy whispers to Morley. Morley takes the sinew and creeps up on Catherine, holding it out and singing "Bobby's Girl"

Catherine (*angrily*) Get off, Morley.

Morley is taken aback. Andy continues whistling

Which colour? (*She holds up two lipsticks*)

Morley does not respond

Morley.

He ignores her

Andy We could chop its head off and mount it on a piece of wood like a trophy.
Catherine Do you like this colour, Morley?
Morley No.
Catherine This one?
Morley Yeah.
Catherine OK. (*She starts to put on the lipstick*)

Morley watches her

Morley David Buckingham is going to the fancy dress.
Catherine You wish you were coming?
Morley Mum will be here.
Catherine Of course.
Morley Do you wish you were going, Andy?
Andy No.
Morley Anyway, Andy's taking me to the fair next week, so there.
Catherine I think you were right about the colour.
Morley You have to do that now on a piece of paper. (*He presses his lips together*)

Catherine You want to try it?

Morley giggles

Andy There you are, Morley. (*He holds up the rabbit's foot*)
Catherine Do you?

Morley giggles again

Andy Will we stretch the skin out to dry?
Catherine Would suit you. Come here.

Morley approaches. Catherine puts the lipstick on him

Andy Will we, Morley?
Morley Yeah.
Catherine There. Look.

Morley looks in the mirror

   Andy once put on all my make-up.

Morley giggles

   Want some eye-shadow?
Morley OK.
Catherine Here. (*She applies the eye-shadow*) Keep still. (*She finishes*)

He wants to look in the mirror

   Wait. (*She puts mascara on his eyelashes*) There. What do you think?

He shrugs

   Show Andy.
Andy Very nice.

   Frank enters

Frank You seen Dad?

Catherine Is he no up at the well?

Frank Been up there. He owes me my wages.

Catherine Oh dear.

Frank He's cashed the milk cheque and he hasn't given me anything. (*To Morley*) What are you doing?

Morley Putting on Cathy's make-up.

Frank shakes his head

Can I put on your ear-rings?

Catherine Which ones?

Morley The sparkly ones.

Catherine OK.

Morley exits

I could lend you some money.

Frank No. I'll get it off him.

Catherine Mebbe he needs it.

Frank But he always does it, you see, Cathy.

Catherine Uh-huh.

Frank You never know what you're going to get from one day to the next. I'm trying to save up to buy a car, see. Saw a little Morris in Westcott's garage in town. Needs a new throttle, new gasket, but I could do that meself. Mr Westcott only wants seventy-five quid for it. He said if I did a few jobs for him I could have it for less.

Catherine Will your dad no buy it for you?

Frank Don't know about that.

Pause

Better go and get washed.

Catherine Cannae wait to see your costume.

Frank laughs

I still think you should be going as Ringo.

Frank I'm not that ugly.

Catherine How dare you!

Frank You seen the nose on him?
Catherine Away wi' you.

Frank exits singing the lines about a rabbit's foot from "Good Luck Charm"

Catherine returns to the mirror

Holding the knife, Andy stands looking at her. They stare at each other

You smell. You havenae washed for weeks.
Andy Have you done it wi' him yet?

She does not reply

Cannae be very comfortable doing it in that car of his. Not like that nice flat Mr Capaldi got you. With that great big double bed in it.
Catherine I left some scones in the oven.

She exits

Andy looks at the knife. He pulls his shirt up. Slowly he draws the blade along his stomach

Catherine enters

She looks at him. She takes the knife from him

I thought you were over that.
Andy They used to shut me up in a dark room when I did it at the home. You could do that.
Catherine Please, Andy.
Andy You're just like everyone else. Mum and Dad didnae want me. My foster parents didnae want me. The Navy didnae want me. And now you don't want me.
Catherine That's no true.
Andy It is. (*He starts to cry*)

She comforts him

Catherine Don't, Andy.
Andy I don't know why you came down here this summer.
Catherine I was worried about you.

Slowly, his tears subside

Let me see that! (*She dabs at the cut with a handkerchief and applies the cream she used on Rob's sting*)
                        The second wee craw
                        Fell and broke his jaw
                        Fell and broke his jaw
                        Fell and broke his jaw aw aw aw *etc.*
Andy You used to say you'd run away wi' me to Australia.
Catherine I'll always look after you. You know that.

Andy does not respond

Don't you?
Andy Do you love me, though?
Catherine Of course I do.

Morley enters, wearing ear-rings and high heels

They look at him. Catherine laughs. Andy starts laughing as well

You look great, Morley.
Andy You lookin' for me, Lily?
Morley Who's Lily?
Andy She's a bar girl at the Silver Dollar Saloon.

He dances with Morley, singing "She'll Be Coming Round the Mountain"

Robert enters

Oooh. There's a stranger just rode into town.
Morley My name's Lily. Hallo.

They laugh

What are you doing in our saloon?

Robert The name is Bond. James Bond.

Catherine straightens his bow tie. Andy whispers in Morley's ear. Morley walks up to Robert "seductively"

Morley Hallo, James.

They laugh

   Would you like a drink of beer?
Robert Scotch on the rocks.
Morley Kiss me, James.
Robert Get off.
Morley I'm not a spy.
Robert Stop it, Morley.
Morley Kiss me.
Robert Stop it.

He pushes Morley away

Morley Aowwhhh.

Andy laughs

Catherine You look great.
Robert Thanks.

   Eileen enters

The others look at her for a moment. They all burst out laughing

Eileen What's so funny?
Andy You look like the BVM.
Morley What's the BVM?
Andy The Blessed Virgin Mary. (*He crosses himself in front of her*)
Morley You look silly.
Eileen Hark who's talking. You'd better get that off. Mum will be here
   soon.
Morley I want her to see it. I look better than you.

Robert You can't go like that.
Catherine You look fine, Eileen.
Eileen What's wrong with it?
Robert Lend her your dressing-gown, Cathy. She could go as a geisha
  girl.

Morley grabs Eileen's shawl and puts it over his head

Morley I'm a ratty ratface and I'm the BVM.
Eileen Give it back.

Morley refuses

  Morley. (*She smacks Morley*)
Morley What's wrong with you? Just because Cathy's costume is better
  than yours.
Eileen Give it back.

She grabs the shawl. He pulls her hair

  Let go.
Morley No.

She grabs his hair

Eileen Let go.
Morley You let go.
Eileen Not until you do.
Morley Well, I'm not going to.
Robert Stop it. Both of you. Morley!
Morley I'm not letting go. Aowwwhhh.
Eileen Let go, then.
Morley No.

They crash around

Eileen Nasty little brat.
Morley Ugly old maid.
Robert Stop it.

Frank (*off*) Give it to me.
George (*off*) You just calm down.
Frank (*off*) It's my money.
George (*off*) You'll get it.

Morley and Eileen stop fighting. Sound of doors slamming

Catherine Frank wants his wages.
Robert He's got money.
Catherine It's no fair, Robert.
Robert You should see. He's got a bank account with fifty quid in it.
Catherine Ay, well, that's his savings.
Andy Have tae get the union on to your dad.
Catherine If Frank does the milking he should get the money.
Eileen We don't need outsiders coming and telling us what to do.

George enters with the pot in his hand

George What?
Robert Nothing.
George I had to buy piping and get it laid.
Catherine Could you no let Frank have some of the log money?
George Need that to buy taps and jubilee clips.
Robert Trouble with Frank is he's like an old miser. He's always got money when he needs a new shirt or a part for his scooter.
Catherine Mebbe that's because he's good with money. Doesnae mean he shouldnae get his wages.

Frank enters

Frank Let me have it.
George (*holding out the pot*) You keep away.
Frank Bloody bastard.
Eileen Frank!
Frank What? You're all on his bloody side.
Catherine Give him some log money.
George He's not having that. Let me have it, Rob.

Robert hesitates

Come one.
Robert Tidn fair, Dad.
George Give it to me.
Robert No, Dad.

Robert gives Frank a pound note. George snatches it from Frank

Dad!
George He's not having it.
Robert Give it to him.
George This is my money. Those logs came off my land.

Robert takes the money back and gives it to Frank

Frank exits

(*To Catherine*) Now, look, I'm not having people coming here and
interfering.
Robert Don't talk to her like that.
George You keep quiet, son.
Catherine It was Frank's money.
George You got a lot to learn, young lady.
Catherine I already know what's fair.
George You don't know anything.
Catherine Here, take your bloody money.

She gets a pound note from her purse and holds it out to George

Robert Don't, Cathy. You earned that.
Catherine I don't mind. Here.

George takes Catherine's money

Catherine exits

Robert You mean old bugger.

Robert tries to snatch the money back. The pot spills. The note tears

Morley Ughhhh.

Robert Now look what you've done.
Eileen Cathy should mind her own business.
Andy What d'ye mean?
Eileen Thinks she can tell us all what to do.
Andy Don't worry, we willnae stick around. We don't need you.
Eileen Go, then.
Morley Elly!

Andy exits

Morley follows him

Eileen gets her purse

Robert You're pathetic, Eileen. (*To George*) Give me the other half.
Eileen (*offering a pound note to George*) Here, Dad.
Robert Give it to me.

George refuses

Eileen Give her this one. Seeing as you're so worried about her. (*She gives Robert her note*)

He takes it and throws the torn half into the chamber pot

Robert Hope you're satisfied.

Robert exits

George fishes the note from the pot

Eileen takes the pot and exits

George is left alone, drying the wet half of the note

Eileen enters with the bucket and a floor-cloth

She starts cleaning up. George is trying to put the note back together. A car drives up outside. George looks out the window

George Your mother's here.

SCENE 4

All, except Frank, are seated around the tea table

Peggy I'll never forget it. He was only three years old, weren't you, Morley? He stood up in front of the whole congregation and said it so loud and clear. What was it about? 'Bout a little boy in Africa who found Jesus, wasn't it? And the preacher pointed to all the other kids in the Sunday School and said "You're all the cake, and this one," and he pointed to Morley, "this one's the cherry on the top". It's true, Catherine.

Catherine I believe you.

Peggy Course, he's always been clever. Learnt to read way before he went to school. I always remember Robert bringing one of his books back from school and not being able to read one of the words and Morley told him what it said. Didn't he, Rob?

Robert Mmmmm.

Peggy Course, George says he takes after his family. No-one else can have any brains. He forgets that my father was a very clever man. He was a butcher. Ran his own business. And my mum was a wonderful speller. She won a prize for spelling. Course she came from a very educated family. Her uncle was Lord Mayor, mind. What do you think of that?

Catherine Amazing.

Peggy Morley looks just like him. Same eyes.

Catherine Right.

Peggy Now he's going to grammar school.

Catherine I know.

Peggy Course, Eileen did quite well, went to grammar school. But Rob was hopeless.

Catherine Mebbe he wasnae encouraged enough.

Peggy He wasn't interested.

George He learnt all he had to learn.

Morley Mum.

Peggy What?

Morley Do I have to wear short trousers?

Peggy What do you mean?

Morley To grammar school.

Peggy What does it say on the form?

Morley It says you can wear long or short.

Eileen All the boys wear short trousers until the second or third years.

Morley David Buckingham isn't.

Eileen Don't start, Morley.

Peggy What is he going to wear?

Eileen Rob's old ones.

Peggy They had holes in them.

Eileen I've cut them off and taken them in.

Peggy He ought to have new trousers for a new school.

Morley See.

Peggy Mr Buckingham wouldn't have his son going to school in cast-offs.

George When we've got this well built there'll be plenty of money. You'll be able to do cream teas without the health inspector coming snooping.

Peggy I'm not doing cream teas. I've already got a job, thank you.

George Cathy'll help out, won't you, Cathy?

Catherine I don't know.

Morley Andy, look. (*He blows down his straw*)

Andy Ay.

George She's a good little worker, this one.

Peggy See, Cathy, that's what he wants. Someone he can leave at home working while he goes off to market gallivanting.

George You haven't got anything to complain about.

Peggy Hear that? I haven't got anything to complain about. What do you think of this house, Catherine?

Catherine It's great.

Peggy What?

Catherine Well... I mean ... it's got a lot of potential.

Peggy It might have potential. What do you think of it as it is?

Catherine I suppose it's a wee bit basic.

Peggy You've hit the nail on the head there, Catherine. Hear that? She can see what this house is like. It's basic. I'd say it was verging on the primitive, wouldn't you, Catherine?

Catherine Well...

Peggy No water. No proper electricity. No comfort. No nothing.

George She's an ungrateful woman, Catherine.

Peggy You leave Catherine out of this.

George Cathy and I understand one another, don't we, Cathy?

Catherine Do we?

George You had one of her scones yet? Be able to sell these with a bit of clotted cream. Make a fortune.

Peggy Who made the sponge?

Eileen I did.

Peggy Sunk in the middle, hasn't it?

Morley blows down the straw again

Eileen Stop it, Morley.
Morley All right, ratty ratface.
George So you gonna come up and see it?
Peggy What?
George The well.
Morley Mum.
Peggy I don't want to see a well.
Morley Will you come up and look at Andy's painting?
Peggy What do I want to see a well for?
Morley Will you, Mum?
Peggy What?
Morley Andy's done a painting on my bedroom wall. Will you come and look at it?
Peggy What do you mean, on the wall?
Andy It's a mural.
Peggy A what?
Andy A mural.
Morley It's a cowboy on a horse. He copied it from a book he's got. He's a really good drawer, Mum. The horse looks real.
Peggy I thought you didn't like cowboy stories.
Morley I do.
Peggy We only papered that room last year.

Pause

Terrible smell of Dettol in here.
Morley That's 'cause Dad spilt his——
Eileen Shut up, Morley.

Pause. Morley blows down his straw

Catherine Frank's no going to have time for his tea if he doesnae hurry up.
Peggy What time does this dance start?
Robert Eight.

Eileen We don't have to be there till nine.

Peggy You don't want to be late.

Eileen We'll have hardly seen you.

Peggy You don't have to worry about me. You go off and enjoy yourselves.

Pause

You going like that?

Eileen Yes.

Peggy You ought to go as Christine Keeler.

Eileen Why?

Peggy Topical, isn't it?

George You know what they say about Christine Keeler, don't you?

Peggy All right, all right. We don't want to hear any of your filth.

George She was up to her neck in champagne...

Peggy That's enough, George.

George And he was up to his arse in cider.

Peggy Really!

George Get it, Cathy?

Catherine Oh. Ay.

Morley I don't. Do you, Andy?

Peggy He's got a dirty mind, Cathy.

Morley Why was it cider?

Eileen Shut up, Morley.

Morley Shut up, Morley.

Peggy I don't know what the world's coming to. There's no standards any more. He was a government minister, mind. And she was sleeping with the Russians. Had a bloomin' KGB man as well as him. Never heard anything like it. That bloke who took the overdose, who was her whatchymecallit, pimp, what was his name? He was the son of a vicar. Just shows, though, doesn't it? They pretend to be so whiter than white all of 'em. And underneath they're as bad as anyone else. Worse.

Eileen S'pose everyone's got skeletons in their cupboards.

Catherine looks at her

Peggy What's that supposed to mean?

Frank enters in his Elvis costume

Catherine Wow. Look at you.

Frank sings three lines of "Rock a Hula"

It's great, Frank.

Frank Thank you.

Robert Your face doesn't look much like Elvis.

Catherine That doesnae matter. It's the spirit of it he's got. Frank takes
    after you more than his dad.

Peggy Mmmmm.

Catherine The rest of the family's quite tall.

Peggy Pass him some bread and butter, Morley.

Catherine No that Frank's short. It's just that his dad and Rob are quite
    tall. And Frank's sort of medium height.

Peggy More trifle, Morley?

Eileen He's already had two lots.

Morley Yes, please.

Catherine Was your father tall?

Peggy He was fairly tall.

Catherine It's funny that, i'n't it?

Peggy Mmmmm.

Pause

Catherine My faether's quite tall.

Eileen Is your father tall, Andy?

Andy Ay.

George I want you to get the pump going, Frank.

Frank You'll be lucky. I'm not going upover in this. Haven't got time
    anyway.

George Won't take a minute. Want to show your mother the water
    running into the tank in the barn.

Frank Let me have me wages, then I might.

Peggy Don't talk to him like that, Frank.

Robert Before we go…

Peggy What?

Robert I got something to say.

Morley Andy, look. (*He opens his mouth and shows Andy the contents*)

Andy laughs

Peggy Morley!
Robert I want a partnership in the farm.
Eileen (*impatiently*) Ohhh.
Robert What?
Eileen Nothing. Do you want some more tea, Dad?
Peggy Stop fussing over him. "You all right, Daddy?"

Eileen goes into the kitchen

Robert I've got some stuff about it from the solicitor. We should get it
   sorted out.
George There's plenty of time for that.
Robert The sooner we do it the better.
Peggy Why?
Robert Death duties.

Morley is showing Andy the contents of his mouth

Peggy Morley!

Andy opens his mouth at Morley

   (*To Andy*) Don't encourage him, please.

Andy and Morley try to suppress their giggles

   There's more than just you to be considered, you know. There's Eileen
   and Morley. And I don't want to be left with nothing.

Eileen enters with the teapot

Robert He's always promised me this farm.
Peggy I don't want to be dependent on you once he's dead.
Eileen Do we have to talk about this now?
Robert When else are we going to talk about it?
Peggy I know you, Robert. You'll just spend it all once you've got it. Look
   at that car. The amount of petrol that must use. You don't need a car like
   that. Spend, spend, spend. That's you.
Morley He bought Cathy a ring.

Peggy Did he?
Morley Yeah. She's wearing it on that chain around her neck.

Silence

Robert It's an engagement ring.
Peggy Well, let's see it, then.

Catherine takes it off the chain and hands it round

Very nice. What are those little stones?
Robert Diamonds.
Peggy Mmmm.
Eileen It's lovely.
Peggy Well, congratulations.
Frank Yeah, congratulations, Cathy. Good luck to you.
Catherine Thanks, Frank.
Peggy I never got an engagement ring. That's the sort of husband I had.
Morley Are you going to come and live here?
Catherine I don't know.
Peggy If you've any sense you'll get as far away from here as possible.
  Take it from me, Catherine. I know. You don't want to end up living
  here. We lived with George's family when we got married. His sister,
  Pam, was always interfering. Never works out.
Robert That's why I want to get it all settled legally.
Eileen I'm sure Cathy doesn't want to listen to all this.
Robert You don't understand. If we don't get it sorted out we could lose
  half this place when he dies.
Eileen Why don't you just push him in his grave?
Robert Don't be so bloody daft. We know why you don't want to talk
  about it. You're bloody jealous, that's your trouble.
Eileen And you can't see what's going on in front of your eyes.
Peggy Why anyone should want to marry into this family I don't know.
Eileen Shut up! Just shut up!

Andy exits

Morley gets up

Peggy What do you say?

Morley Please can I leave the table?
Peggy Mustn't forget your manners. Go on.

Morley exits

Don't you ever talk to me like that. Telling me I've got skeletons in my
cupboard.
Eileen I didn't say that.
Peggy I know you and your little jibes. "Everyone's got skeletons in their
cupboards." Sitting there with that little smile on your face. But
underneath you're being catty. That's just like his sister, Pam. Your
father's the one with skeletons in his cupboard. Not me. I haven't got
any skeletons.
George How many men would take a wife back after she's jumped into
bed with another man and had a kid by him?
Peggy That's right; throw that up again. You do anything wrong and it
gets thrown up to you for the rest of your life. Course, you don't talk
about what you've done.

Frank starts to leave quietly

George I haven't done anything.
Peggy Oh, no? You know what he did, Catherine, while I was in hospital
having Robert?
Eileen Stop it!

Frank has gone

Peggy My sister, Lily, came and looked after him, and you know what he
did?
George Lily knows what happened. You ask her.
Peggy He slept with my own sister. That's what your beloved Daddy did.
That's the sort of man he is.
George That sort of thing runs in your family.
Peggy And what do you mean by that?
George You know. All the women in your family have the same
weakness. Your sister Lily's like it. Your precious mother was no better.
Peggy You leave my mother out of this.
George The Lord Mayor's niece had to get married from what I heard. She
was pregnant when she married your father.

Peggy How dare you.

George Then there was Manfred. She went off with a bloody POW, Catherine. Had a little Jerry bastard.

Peggy I'll kill you.

Catherine starts to go

George You stay here. You might learn something.

Catherine stays

Peggy Ohhh! (*She throws Morley's flowers and then food at George*)

Eileen Mum!

Peggy Don't you "Mum" me. You think the same as him. You all take his side. He's a dirty old man and a liar. (*She goes to hit George*)

George holds her hands. They struggle

Eileen Dad! Mum! Don't!

Morley runs on

Morley Leave her alone. Leave her alone! (*He kicks George*)

Eileen Morley, stop it.

George (*to Peggy*) You behave yourself. This is what she gets like, Cathy. Hysterical.

Eileen Dad.

Peggy cries

Robert Let's go.

Catherine hesitates

Get your coat.

Catherine exits

Robert follows her out

George You come and look at this well.
Eileen Leave her, Dad.

George and Eileen exit

Morley It's all right, Mum.
Peggy Your mother's a bad woman, Morley.
Morley You're not. You're not.
Peggy You say that now. But one day you'll think it like the rest of them.
Morley I won't. I love you.
Peggy I know. (*She hugs him*) Would you like to meet Bill?
Morley All right.
Peggy He's been very good to me. He looks after me.
Morley I'll look after you.
Peggy Would you like to come and live with us?
Morley Where?
Peggy In St Leonards.
Morley Where's that?
Peggy In Sussex. Near Aunty Lily.

Pause

Well?
Morley Dunno. Where would I go to school?
Peggy There's a nice school in Hastings...
Morley I wouldn't know anybody.
Peggy You'd soon make friends.

Pause

You think about it.
Morley OK.
Peggy Bill's taking me down to Cornwall. We're going down there to stay
   with his mother for the week. You could come with us.
Morley When?
Peggy Tonight. Be a little holiday before you start school.
Morley Tonight?
Peggy Yes.
Morley Andy's taking me to the fair this week.

Peggy I expect there's a fair in Cornwall.
Morley We were going to have a camp-fire and cook our rabbit.
Peggy Oh.
Morley And we haven't finished the mural.
Peggy I see.
Morley I promised.
Peggy Oh, well...

Frank enters

Frank You want a lift into town?
Peggy I'm not riding on that scooter. I'll get a lift with Rob.
Frank He's gone.
Peggy Oh.
Frank So, you coming?
Peggy In a minute.
Frank I'm going now.
Peggy Don't hurry me. (*She applies lipstick to her lips*)
Frank I thought Bill was waiting for you in the *Rose and Crown*.
Peggy I don't know why you hang around here. There's nothing for you here. I don't know why you don't join the army or something. Do something useful with your life.
Frank Morley going with you?
Peggy You go and start up the scooter. I'm coming.

Frank exits

Peggy blots her lips with a piece of paper

Morley I don't want you to go, Mum.
Peggy It won't be for long. You can come to St Leonards and visit.
Morley All right.
Peggy So don't cry.

He shakes his head

You have your camp-fire and go to the fair.

He hugs her. Sound of a scooter starting up

I'd better go, love. Be a good boy.

She kisses him and exits

Sound of a scooter revving and driving away. Morley picks up the flowers and puts them in the vase

SCENE 5

The yard. There is a pipe coming out of the ground

Andy, George and Morley are bending over it. Morley is wearing Andy's cowboy hat

Morley Is it coming?
George No. (*He sucks on the pipe*)
Morley What you doing?
George Seeing if I can suck it through.
Andy Do ye no need a pump on the tank?
George No, gravity does it, see. That's why we put the tank up in the loft.
Andy You're a very clever man.
George That's true, lad.
Andy Mebbe there's a blockage somewhere.
Morley Will it take much longer, Dad?
George Is the tap on?
Andy I think so. I'll get something to poke down there. (*He finds a stick which he pokes down the pipe*)
Morley Dad!
George What, boy?
Morley Andy and me are going to the fair tonight, you know.
George Just get this done.
Morley Eileen won't let me stay out very late. 'Cause of school tomorrow.
Andy D'ye no want to see the water running, Morley?
Morley Yeah.
Andy I think there might be something down there.

Robert enters. His hands are covered in oil

Morley We're connecting up the water.

George Can't get it to come through.

Robert ignores them and exits

Morley How long will it take them?
George What?
Morley To get to Scotland tomorrow?
George Bloody hours.
Morley He said they're going to see Loch Lomond.

Andy and George do not respond

Do you wish you were going, Andy?
Andy No.
George You're going to stay and work for me, aren't you, son? Need a good strong bloke like you. Bloke with brains. Make a farmer of you, won't I?
Andy Ye really think so?
George Course I do.
Andy I wouldnae mind trying.
George I'll see you're all right.
Morley (*singing*)   "You take the high road
                              And I'll take the low road
                              And I'll be in Scotland before you --"
George Quiet, boy.
Andy Will I go and check the tap?
George Good idea.

Andy exits

Morley Have you ever been to Scotland, Dad?
George Nothing to see up there.

Robert enters, carrying a tyre

Rob!
Robert What?
George Come and see if you can get this water to come through.
Robert Thought you had all the help you needed.

George Won't take you a minute.

Robert comes and takes the pipe. He looks down it, then sucks

Morley Ughhhh! Dad's been sucking that.

Robert takes it out of his mouth, wipes it and sucks again

Robert Nothing.

He hands the pipe back to George

George Go up to the loft and see if Andy's got it connected right.
Robert I gotta get this car done tonight.
George Where d'ee get that tyre?
Robert Old Wolsey in the field.
George I was going to put that one on my car.
Robert Too bad.
George (*taking hold of the tyre*) Hey boy, come on, no need to be like that.
Robert Get off.
George You go and give Andy a hand.
Robert Cow's probably stepped on the pipe in the orchard. You haven't
    hardly buried it.
George It'll be all right.
Robert Come winter you won't have no water 'cause the pipes'll be
    frozen.
George I know what I'm doing.
Robert Oh, yeah, course you do.
George Come on, son. You and me don't want to fall out. Don't want to
    let her come between us.
Robert Tidn her. Can't you get that into your thick head? It's you. When
    I was his age you used to take me up over and point to it all and say, "One
    day, all this will be yours, boy". Soon as I want a share in it you won't
    let me have it.
George We'll sort something out.
Robert (*almost pleading*) Phone up the solicitor, then.
George You don't want to let no solicitors start taking over. End up taking
    all your money off you.
Robert Get your two new mechanical diggers to do it for you. You can
    give your bloody farm to Morley.

George Rob! Rob!
Robert Arsehole! (*He is not calling George an arsehole but saying the word as an oath*)
George Piss!
Robert (*answering him*) Shit!

Robert exits

George returns to the pipe

Morley Can I have my money, Dad?
George What for?
Morley The fair.
George Haven't got any tonight.
Morley You promised you'd let me have some if we helped you.
George You'll get it, lad.

Sound of the scooter

Morley Elly! Frank! We're connecting up the water.
George Frank! Frank!
Morley He's putting his scooter away.

Eileen enters. She has a crash helmet on

Andy and I are helping Dad.
Eileen Tap working in the house yet?
George Haven't got it running out the tank. Shouldn't be long. Need Frank to go up and help Andy get it running. He's s'posed to have fitted the pipe onto the stopcock.
Eileen What's Rob doing?
Morley He won't help us. He's getting the car ready for tomorrow. Elly, will you let me have some money?
Eileen What for?
Morley I'm going to the fair with Andy.
Eileen You ought to be getting ready for school.
Morley I'm going to the fair.
Eileen Don't know what you're going to do next week. Frank's got this job. Rob'll be away.

Morley And I'll be at school.
George I've asked Andy to stay on.
Eileen Oh. Don't know if that's a good idea.
Morley Course it is. You don't know anything.

Pause

Eileen What if he doesn't come back?
George He'll be back.
Eileen They're talking about emigrating.
George You ask Derek Rudd if he'll help out with the combining?
Eileen His father won't let him.
George Why not?
Eileen You still haven't paid him for last year.
George I'll pay him.

Pause

Eileen What did you think of Mum when you married her?
George What do you mean?
Eileen Had she had other boyfriends and things?
George She wadn a virgin. Know that now.
Eileen Would you have married her if you'd known?
George I dunno. I'll go up and see old Rudd.
Eileen No.
George Why not?
Eileen Don't start pestering Derek's father.
George It's all in the family now, idn it?
Eileen I don't want you to.

Pause

  We don't know anything about Cathy and Andy.
George What's that s'posed to mean?
Eileen Nothing.

  Andy enters

Andy I cannae do it.

George What's up?
Andy That tap willnae move.
George You put some oil on it?
Andy Ay.
George Frank! Frank!
Frank (*off*) Coming.
George Need your help.

Frank sings two lines of "As Long as He Needs Me" off stage

Andy How'd it go?
Frank (*off*) What?
Andy Your first day.

Frank enters, wearing his crash helmet and carrying a single

Frank They had me changing the oil on the vet's car. Told Westcott I
    thought it was missing. Didn't believe me. Then we listened to the
    engine. He said, "I think you'm right, boy". Was too. Needed a new
    spark plug. Said to me after: "You'll be an asset, boy, I can see that".
George I want you to get this tap turned on.
Frank Only just got back. Gotta milk the cows yet.

Catherine enters

Catherine Frank, can we borrow your Stillson? We cannae get the wheel
    nuts off.
Frank It's in my tool-box.
Catherine We couldnae find your tool-box.
Morley That's because he hides it in the loft.
Frank Here. Look what I got today. (*He shows Catherine his single*)
Catherine It's out, then.
Frank Released it yesterday.
Morley What is it?

Frank taps his nose

George Come and have a look at the tank.

George exits

Frank Won't be a minute, Cathy. (*He sings four lines of "As Long as He Needs Me"*)

Frank exits

Catherine (*to Andy*) I'm making chips for dinner the night.

Andy does not respond

Andy's favourite meal. I'n't it?
Morley He's not talking to you. Anyway, we're going to the fair.
Catherine (*to Andy*) Hope you're going tae have a wash first.
Andy Come on, Morley, let's go and help your dad.

Andy and Morley leave

Catherine Your dad and Andy seem to be getting on.
Eileen Mmmm. (*She looks up at the birds*)
Catherine That's those birds again.

Eileen does not respond

There's a lot of them the night.

Pause

My hands. They're covered in oil.
Eileen What time you going in the morning?
Catherine Early.

Pause

Look, it's no me. It's Robert who wants tae go.
Eileen Mmm.
Catherine I like it here.
Eileen Don't know how much longer I'll be here.
Catherine No?
Eileen Derek's asked me to marry him.
Catherine Ay. Robert told me.

Eileen Oh.
Catherine Congratulations.
Eileen Mmmmmm?
Catherine If it's what you want.
Eileen You can't spend your whole life looking for the perfect person.
Catherine I think there's someone out there for everyone.
Eileen Honesty's the most important thing in any marriage.

Robert enters

Robert Got that Stillson?
Catherine He's gone tae get it.

Robert kisses Catherine

Robert Idn she lovely? Thank my lucky stars nobody gave her a lift that
   night. (*To Eileen*) What you lookin' at?
Eileen The house-martins. They're restless.

Robert and Catherine look

Robert They're just getting ready to fly off to Africa or wherever it is they
   go to.

*They look up. Pause. Robert kisses Catherine. Eileen cries softly. The
other two stop kissing and look at her. Robert laughs. Catherine digs him
in the ribs to make him stop. They look at the birds*

Frank enters

Frank They were trying to turn that tap the wrong way. (*He stops to see
   what they're looking at*) Ought to get those nests knocked out. (*He
   hands Robert the spanner*) Make sure you give it back. Don't go driving
   off with it tomorrow.

Morley runs on

Morley Is it coming through? They've got the tap turned on.
Frank Not yet.

Morley What's wrong with you?
Eileen Nothing.
Morley You been crying?
Robert Hold it in the bucket.

Frank does so

Catherine Is it blocked?

Frank looks down the pipe

   Don't.

Frank puts the pipe back in the bucket

Robert Let's see.
Catherine Careful.

   Andy runs on

Andy Is it coming through?

Robert takes the pipe and looks down it. The water shoots into his face. The others laugh. He puts his finger over the hole and squirts it at them

Frank Get off.

Robert pursues them

Eileen Don't be silly, Rob. These are my clothes for work.
Robert All right. (*He puts the pipe back in the bucket*) It's all right.
   Honest.

The others approach

Frank How strong is it? (*He leans in to feel the water*)

Robert takes the pipe and squirts water at him again

   Aowwhh. Get off!

Robert squirts it at the others. They scream. Andy runs up to Robert and tries to get the pipe from him. They struggle. Catherine gets the bucket. Whilst the other two are fighting, she comes up behind them and pours the bucket over them. Robert squirts water. He misses Catherine and gets Eileen

Eileen I told you not to do that. (*She pounds furiously on his back with her fists*)
Robert Sorry.

Andy grabs him from behind. Robert slips. Andy kicks him ferociously

Catherine Andy!
Frank Hey, come on, Andy.
Catherine Andy, stop it. Stop it
Frank Here, Andy, mate. That's enough now.

Catherine and Frank pull Andy off Robert. Robert is curled up

George enters

George What's going on?
Eileen You all right? Rob?
George Go and turn the tap off, Morley. Use the wrench.

Morley exits

Catherine goes to Robert and helps him up

Robert Bit winded. You won't get her back like that.

Robert picks up the spanner and exits

Catherine follows him

Frank Better get those cows milked.

He exits

George (*quietly, to Eileen, so that Andy can't hear*) What's going on?

Eileen Leave it.
George You know something I don't?
Eileen It's probably all for the best, anyway.

She exits

The water stops

George Can get this joined up now. Give me your screwdriver, boy.

Andy gives him the screwdriver. George starts to join the two ends of the pipe

You don't want to lose your head like that, lad.

Andy cries

> "If you can keep your head when all about you,
> Are losing theirs and blaming it on you.
> You'll be a man, my son, you'll be a man." (*He screws on the pipe*)

All my life I've been surrounded by people who don't appreciate me. Many's the time I could have given up. Sat down and cried. But you gotta keep your head, you see.

Andy nods

Morley runs on

Morley Can we go to the fair now?
George Go and turn it on again.
Morley I've just turned it off. Andy, can we go?
George (*to Andy*) Just go and turn it on again, lad.
Morley Aren't we going to the fair?
George Won't take a minute.
Morley Andy.
Andy I don't really want to tonight, Morley.
Morley But it finishes tonight.
Andy Stop going on, Morley. Will you leave me alone! You're a bloody pest!

Andy exits

Pause

George How about you and me going to the fair, lad?

Morley does not respond

   'Member going to the fair with my old dad.
Morley Andy was going to take me on the waltzer.
George I'll take you on the waltzer.
Morley Tonight?
George Course.

Pause

   You spent a lot of time with Andy, haven't you?
Morley Yes.
George And Cathy.
Morley Mmmm.
George What do they get up to?
Morley What do you mean?
George Just wondered.
Morley Does Andy love Cathy?
George What do you think?
Morley I saw them kissing in the loft once.

They laugh

   And...
George What?
Morley I don't think I should tell you.
George Come on, lad. Course you can. (*He waits*)
Morley In Andy's cowboy book...
George Yeah.
Morley He's written his name.
George And?
Morley His surname isn't Mullen like he said.
George Oh.

Morley It's MacCusker. Like Cathy's...
George I see.
Morley It says this book belongs to Andrew James MacCusker.
George Right.
Morley Do you think they're married?
George I don't know.

Pause. George takes a coin from his pocket

   Here's some spending money.
Morley I don't want it.
George Go on. You'll need it. All those rides.

   Peggy enters and watches them unseen

Morley Did they have waltzers when you were a little boy?
George Had the old carousel. And the rifle range. My dad won me a toy
   gun. Had it for years. And we went in to see the man with two heads.
Morley You won't tell, will you? About Andy.
George Course I won't.

Morley takes the money

Morley Did he really have two heads?
George Saw it with my own eyes.

George puts his arm around Morley. They laugh

Peggy What's going on?

Morley starts, guilty that she has seen him sharing intimacy with George

Morley Mum!
George Where've you come from?
Peggy Just walked up from the station.
Morley You come home?
Peggy Here. I've brought you something. (*She gives him a bag*)
Morley What is it?
Peggy Have a look.

Morley Is it trousers? It's long trousers.

Eileen enters

Eileen Mum!
Peggy No need to look so shocked. Everyone's looking at me as if I've just got off the sputnik
Morley Mum's bought me some long trousers.
Eileen The house is in a mess. Your bed hasn't got clean sheets.
George She can sleep in my bed.
Peggy Don't you start.

Andy enters

Andy Oh, hi.
Peggy Still here, then.
Andy Ay.
Morley Cathy and Rob are going to Scotland tomorrow.
Peggy Are they?
Andy The water's running out of the tank but there's nothing running in.
George Ballcock's stuck I spec'.
Peggy Haven't you got it all plumbed in yet?
George You just go indoors and turn the tap on.

George exits with Andy

Eileen Bill drive you?
Peggy No, I came on the coach.
Eileen How long you staying?
Peggy I don't know.
Eileen When's Bill expecting you back?
Peggy How many more questions? (*To Morley*) So are you pleased?
Morley Yeah.
Peggy You still love your mum, then?

Pause

Morley He was just telling me about going to the fair.
Peggy Give me a kiss, then.

Morley kisses her

    Aren't you going to try them on?
Morley OK.
Peggy Put your blazer on as well.

    Morley exits

Eileen Mum.
Peggy What?
Eileen Derek's asked me to marry him.
Peggy Oh.
Eileen You think I should?
Peggy How do I know? Only you can know that. He's dug up my lupins to put that pipe through the garden.

    Catherine enters

Catherine Hallo there.
Peggy I hear you're off to Scotland.
Catherine That's right.
Peggy Best thing you can do.

    Andy enters

Andy Cathy!
Catherine What?
George (*off*) Come back here.
Andy No.

    George enters

Catherine What is it?
George Want a word with you, Cathy.
Catherine Oh ay?
George I want you to tell Rob to unpack his bags.
Catherine We're leaving tomorrow. We're no changing our minds now.
George He belongs here, Cathy.
Catherine He's a grown man. He can make up his own mind.

Peggy Course he can.

Catherine You all make him feel that he's stupid.

George No, we don't.

Catherine Whose fault is it that he cannae read and write properly?

George I'm not going to stand by and see my son throw it all away. I've done all this for him. I'm not having you coming along and taking him off to God-knows-where.

Robert comes in to see what is going on

Catherine He's the one that wants tae leave. No me. Let him have his share and then he'll stay.

George I've worked hard for this house and this land. I'm not giving it away till the time's right.

Robert How much older do I have to be, for God's sake?

George I didn't move into my own farm till I was forty-five. I stayed working for me dad.

Peggy Yeah, and the rows you used to have about it.

George You mustn't run before you've learnt how to walk.

Catherine Well, he's walking. Tomorrow. Out that door.

Frank enters to see what is going on

George And what happens when he finds out about what's been going on?

Catherine What d'ye mean?

George We got eyes, you know.

Catherine I don't know what you're talking about.

Eileen Dad! Don't!

George 'Bout you and your brother here.

Catherine What?

George You and Andy.

Robert Don't be bloody stupid.

George Mucking around in the loft.

Catherine What have you done?

Andy I havenae done anything.

Catherine looks at Eileen

George Morley saw them.

Robert Cathy?

Catherine does not respond

Morley enters

Morley They're a bit long.

They all look at him

Catherine You nasty wee sneak.
Robert Cathy. I don't understand...
Peggy It's disgusting.
Catherine Disgusting? You find me disgusting, do you? And what are
  you? Are you no disgusting? You're bloody hypocrites, the bloody lot
  of yees.

She exits

Robert Cathy!
George You go and unpack your suitcase, Rob. You're better off without
  a woman like that.

Robert advances on George with the spanner

Frank Steady on, Rob.
Robert You bloody bastard...

He picks George up and shakes him

  You bloody bastard.
Eileen Rob.
Robert You bloody bastard. You bloody bastard. (*He punches George*)

Robert exits

Eileen goes to George

Eileen Dad?

George I'm all right.
Morley You said you wouldn't tell.
George Let's see if this tap's running.

He goes into the house

Eileen follows him

Morley I didn't say anything.

Andy hits Morley

Andy You liar.
Morley Andy.
Peggy Here, that's enough of that.
Andy Your wee daughter here is a sneak.
Peggy You can stop that sort of talk.
Andy You didnae think she was your son, did you?
Peggy You want to watch what you're saying. After what you've been up to.
Andy Is the wee girl going to cry.
Peggy Here, I might just contact the naval police.

Pause

Saw them at the railway station. Had a photo of the runaway they were looking for. You'd better get your bags packed. Wouldn't take me long to walk down to the phone box.
Morley Mum! Andy!
Andy Get off me.

Andy exits

Morley sobs

Peggy Come on, Morley. Come in with me.
Morley I don't want to.

He runs away upover

Frank looks at Peggy and exits

SCENE 6

Morley's bedroom that Andy has been using

On the wall is the painting of the cowboy on the horse. Andy is lying on the bed

Catherine enters with Andy's jeans

Catherine I brought these off the line. Will I put them in your rucksack?
Andy I'll wear them.
Catherine Here.
Andy Have tae get a wash first.
Catherine Frank's going to give us a lift up to the garage in the car. This long distance lorry driver he knows will pick us up there.
Andy You don't have tae come wi' me.
Catherine I cannae stay here.
Andy I'm going back to Portsmouth.
Catherine Right.
Andy The reggies will find me in the end. They always do.

Pause

Catherine What will happen to you?
Andy They'll just lock me up for a while. It willnae be for long.
Catherine I could come to Portsmouth wi' you.
Andy No. Go back tae Mr Capaldi. He'll look after ye.
Catherine I'm no going back there.
Andy Where, then?
Catherine I don't know. London.
Andy There's lots of men like Capaldi in London.
Catherine Mebbe.

She touches his hair

Catherine ⎫ *(together)* The third wee craw
Andy   ⎭   Couldnae flee at aw

Couldnae flee at aw
Couldnae flee at aw aw aw aw
The third wee craw
Couldnae flee at aw
On a cold and frosty morning.

Eileen enters

Eileen Oh, sorry. I was looking for Morley.
Andy He's no here.

Andy picks up his towel and exits

Eileen Mum's worried because he ran off upover.

Catherine gets up to go

What are you going to do?
Catherine What do you think I'm going to do? Pack my rucksack. Get out. You must be feeling very pleased with yourself. You never liked me, did you? You were jealous of me right from the start. Now you've got him back.
Eileen (*sharply*) Yes, and you've got Andy.

Pause

Catherine Ay, well, mebbe we've got more in common than you thought.

George enters

George Ah, here you are.
Eileen Get out, Dad.
George I want a word with Cathy.
Eileen Leave her.
George You don't have to go, you know.

Catherine laughs

Rob didn wanna leave here. He couldn live nowhere else.
Catherine Ay well, you're probably right about that.

George Nobody wants you to go. You go out and tell Rob you're staying.

She does not respond

   Rob doesn't want you to go.
Catherine He hasnae said that tae me.

Peggy enters

Peggy Is he up here?
Eileen No.
Peggy Hope he hasn't fallen down that well. (*She goes and opens the window*) Morley! Moooooorley!
George He'll be all right.
Peggy I need some water for the kettle.
George What d'ee mean?
Peggy There's no water coming out the tap.

Peggy and George exit

Eileen Rob's out sitting in his car.
Catherine I know.
Eileen He locked the door when I went out to speak to him.

Pause

   Where will you go?
Catherine Don't know.
Eileen Back to Scotland?
Catherine No. London, mebbe.
Eileen London?
Catherine Ay.
Eileen What will you do there?
Catherine I'll be all right.
Eileen And Andy?
Catherine Back the Navy.
Eileen It's true, then.
Catherine Ay.

Pause

You didnae need Morley to tell you, did you?
Eileen Mmm?
Catherine About me and Andy.
Eileen No.
Catherine Our mum put him in a home when he was ten. He was fifteen
when he came back. My wee lost brother.
Eileen Mmmmmmm.

Pause

Catherine You're doing the right thing.
Eileen What?
Catherine Getting out of here. Marrying Derek.
Eileen Maybe...
Catherine You havenae changed your mind?
Eileen Maybe I'm not the marrying kind.
Catherine You have to get out, Eileen.
Eileen Mmmmm.

Robert enters and stands unseen in the doorway

You'll miss Andy. (*She sees Robert*)

Catherine turns and sees him

Catherine I'll miss Robert.

Pause

Eileen Hallo.

Robert turns and exits

Eileen follows him

*Catherine takes the chain from around her neck. She takes the ring from
it and looks at it*

Eileen returns

He's gone to his bedroom.

Catherine Uh-huh.

Eileen He's so proud. And he's old-fashioned, really. When it comes to women. Wants us to be whiter than white.

Catherine Ay. Well, give him this. (*She holds out the ring*)

Eileen He'll never forgive us, you know.

Catherine Mebbe.

Eileen You could stay...

Catherine Your dad would never let me forget...

Eileen A girl on her own in London. Anything could happen.

Catherine Ay. (*She holds out the ring*)

Eileen takes it

  Morley enters

Eileen There you are. Mum's looking for you. Mum! Mum!

  She exits

Catherine What do you want? Come to get your room back? Don't worry, we'll be gone soon. You won't have many friends in this life, if you carry on being a sneak, you know. D'ye hear me?

Morley nods

  Catherine exits

Morley has the rabbit's foot. He curls up on the bed and strokes it

  Peggy and Eileen enter

Peggy There you are. I've been worried sick about you.

Morley I've been upover.

Peggy Hope you haven't got those trousers dirty.

Morley No.

Peggy Where are his pyjamas?

  Eileen exits

Peggy straightens the bedclothes. She hums a few bars of "Blow the Wind Southerly". Morley strokes the foot

What's that you've got?
Morley Nothing.

Eileen enters with the pyjamas

Peggy (*looking out of the window*) So quiet. Hate the quiet. Makes you feel like you're buried alive.
Eileen Was it quiet in Cornwall?
Peggy What you mean?
Eileen Where Bill s mother lived.
Peggy She's got this great big house in the town. She's a real snob.
Eileen Oh.
Peggy Got Bill under her thumb, as well.
Eileen Yeah?
Peggy Wouldn't do anything without asking her. What sort of man's that?

Frank enters

Frank Andy ready?
Peggy How should I know?
Frank Need to get a move on. Else my mate will have gone.
Eileen I'll go and see what they re doing.

Eileen exits

Peggy So you've got a job.
Frank Yeah.
Peggy 'Bout time you got away from here.
Frank You never wanted me here, did you?
Peggy Don't know what you're talking about.

"Wooden Heart" starts playing in Rob's bedroom

George (*off*) Rob! Rob!
Peggy Leave him alone.
Frank (*calling to Robert*) Be careful with my records!
George (*off*) Rob! Open this door.

George enters

He's put the chair up against the door.

Frank (*calling to Robert*) It's my room, too.

Peggy Is there any water yet?

George Andy's been having a wash and it's caused an air-block, Frank.

Frank What you want me to do about it?

George Need someone to help drain the system.

Frank I'm taking these two up to the garage.

George I was talking to the people from the petrol company the other day.

Peggy What people?

George They reckon I could get permission to build a petrol station in the lower field.

Peggy Where are you going to get the money for that?

George I'd need somebody mechanically-minded to run it. What'ee think?

Peggy You don't know anything about petrol stations.

Frank You wouldn't get me back here. Not if you paid me a million pounds.

Frank exits

Peggy Come on, Morley. Past your bedtime.

George Soon be your bedtime, too.

Peggy Are you going to get this water fixed or not?

George What do I get if I do?

Peggy Get off now, George.

George I want to give you a nice welcome home.

Peggy George...

Morley covers his head with the pillow. George whispers in Peggy's ear

Honestly. Go on.

George exits

Peggy laughs

These pyjamas need airing.

Morley does not respond

So this is the picture.
Morley Yes.
Peggy Mmmm.

Pause

At grammar school you'll have lots of friends. Friends your own age.

Andy enters, and is standing in the doorway with just a towel round him

Peggy exits

Andy takes off his towel. Morley watches. Andy puts on his underpants and then his jeans. "Venus in Blue Jeans" is playing in Rob's bedroom. Andy sits and rubs his hair

Morley I brought you this.

Andy does not respond

It's the rabbit's foot. It will bring you luck. (*He lays it on the bed*)

Andy picks it up and puts it around his neck. Then he looks at the picture

Andy We never finished the picture.

Morley shakes his head. Andy straps up his rucksack. He picks up his cowboy hat

Ye keeping this?

Morley does not answer

Are ye?

Morley nods. Andy throws it on the bed. He looks at Morley. He sits on the bed

Well, pardner, this looks like the end.

Morley does not respond. Andy lies on the bed with Morley

It was great waking up in this bed in the morning. I used tae lie here looking at the ceiling.

Morley looks up

You see where the water comes in and there's all them brown marks?

Morley nods

See that one there?
Morley Which one?
Andy The one that looks like a giraffe.
Morley Yes.

They look at the ceiling

That's a lady's arm.
Andy What—the giraffe?
Morley It's not a giraffe. She's got a long glove on.
Andy What, the neck is her arm?
Morley Yes. She's got her hand like that. (*He puts his arm up*)
Andy Ay, so she has.
Morley She's wearing a dress like a Spanish lady.
Andy Och yes. And there was me thinking that was a bush in the front of the giraffe.

Morley giggles

Well, Matt, I guess I gotta go. Gotta head back into town and hand myself over to the sheriff and his men.
Morley I don't want you to go. (*He curls up beside Andy*)

Andy puts his arm round him. Morley looks at Andy. He kisses Andy

Peggy enters with the pyjamas

Andy and Morley separate

Peggy Here you are, Morley.

Andy puts on his socks and shoes

   Catherine enters

Catherine Ready?
Andy Nearly.
Catherine Hope you enjoy your new school, Morley. (*She gives him her ear-rings*) A keepsake.
Peggy Don't forget your hat.
Morley That's mine.

Peggy puts the hat on the bed

Andy Bye, then.

Catherine hugs Morley. He holds on to her

Catherine We've got to go.
Peggy Morley, let her go. Morley!

Catherine disengages herself

   Frank enters

The Beatles' "She Loves You" plays through to the final curtain

Frank (*calling to Robert*) I haven't played that yet. You be careful with it.
Catherine I knew I'd convert you.
Frank Ready, then?
Peggy He'll wave from the window, won't you, Morley?

Morley nods

   Catherine, Andy and Frank exit

Aren't you going to wave them goodbye?

Morley shakes his head

Shall I bring you up some hot milk?
Morley I don't drink hot milk anymore.
Peggy What do you drink?
Morley Cocoa.
Peggy Shall I make you that?
Morley If you like.

Peggy exits

Morley lies listening. A car starts. Sounds of goodbyes. Morley puts the cowboy hat on and holds the ear-rings up

Robert enters

The car drives off. Robert looks out the window and then sits on the bed

Eileen enters

Eileen They've gone. (*She goes to touch Robert*)
Robert Get off.
Peggy (*off*) Go down and get me some water from the well. That's what you can do.

Eileen looks at the ring

(*Off*) There's no water coming from that tap. Here, turn it on. Now, is there, or isn't there? No, there isn't.
Morley One day I'm leaving here.
Eileen Yes?
Morley Yes.
Peggy (*off*) This is how things always are on this farm. The electric doesn't work. The roof leaks. The bloomin' water doesn't work. Nothing works.

Eileen looks out the window. She holds out her hand

Eileen It's starting to rain. (*She closes the window, then looks at Robert*)

Morley holds the ear-rings up to the light. The cowboy looks down from the picture

"She Loves You" comes to an end

CURTAIN

FURNITURE AND PROPERTY LIST

Further dressing may be added at the director's discretion

SCENE 1

On stage: Table
Battery radio
Aladdin lamp
Funnel
Can of oil
Sewing items
Box of chocolates
Towel
Morley's farm trousers
Petrol can
Piece of hose
Plates and cutlery

Off stage: Saucepan (**Eileen**)
Bucket of milk (**Frank**)
Jug and some muslin (**Frank**)
Pail (**Frank**)

Personal: **Eileen:** purse with money (£1 and ten shilling note)
Morley: keys
Andy: haversack

SCENE 2

Strike: Table
Chairs
Radio
Aladdin lamp
Funnel
Can of oil
Sewing items
Box of chocolates

           Towel
           Petrol can
           Piece of hose
           Plates and cutlery
           Saucepan
           Bucket of milk
           Jug and some muslin
           Pail
           Can

Set: Sandwiches
           Bottle of lemonade
           Catherine's bag. *In it:* tube of cream, coins

Off stage: Mud (**Andy**)
           Postcard (**Eileen**)

Personal: **Catherine:** handkerchief

Scene 3

Strike: Sandwiches
           Bottle of lemonade
           Catherine's bag

Set: Mirror
           Cleaning utensils
           Bucket of water
           Table
           Piece of string
           Eileen's purse. *In it:* pound note

Off stage: Bunch of wild flowers (**Morley**)
           Knife (**Morley**)
           Plate of scones (**Catherine**)
           Bloody knife and rabbit's foot (**Andy**)
           Chamber pot (**George**)
           Bucket of water and a floor-cloth (**Eileen**)

Personal: **Robert:** forms, pound note
           Catherine: make-up, handkerchief, tube of cream, purse with a
             pound note
           Eileen: shawl

SCENE 4

Strike: Chamber pot
            Bucket of water and a floor-cloth

Set: Table
            Chairs
            Food and drinks, as for tea: scones, trifle, glass of lemonade
                with two straws, etc.

Off stage: Teapot (**Eileen**)

Personal: **Morley:** straw
            Catherine: chain with a ring
            Peggy: make-up, tissues

SCENE 5

Strike: Table
            Chairs
            Food and drinks, as for tea: scones, trifle, etc.
            Teapot

Set: Water pipe
            Stick
            Bucket

Off stage: Tyre (**Robert**)
            Single (**Frank**)
            Spanner (**Frank**)
            Screwdriver (**Andy**)
            Bag, *In it:* long trousers (**Peggy**)

Personal: **George:** coin

SCENE 6

Strike: Water pipe
            Stick
            Bucket
            Tyre
            Screwdriver

Set: Bed. *Or. it:* bedclothes, pillow
               Towel
               Underpants
               Rucksack
               Cowboy hat

Off stage: **Andy**'s jeans (**Catherine**)
               Pyjamas (**Eileen**)
               Pyjamas (**Peggy**)
               Ear-rings (**Catherine**)

Personal: **Catherine:** chain with a ring
               Morley: rabbit's foot

LIGHTING PLOT

2 interior and 2 exterior settings

Scene 1

To open: Indoor rainy day effect

Cue 1	**Morley**: "She's not here, though, is she?" *Bring up oil lamp effect*	(Page 2)
Cue 2	**Eileen** turns up the light *Increase oil lamp effect*	(Page 3)
Cue 3	**Eileen** turns up the light *Increase oil lamp effect*	(Page 4)
Cue 4	**Morley** turns the switch *Fade up a flickering light*	(Page 20)

Scene 2

To open: General exterior effect

No cues

Scene 3

To open: Overall indoor lighting

No cues

Scene 4

To open: Overall indoor lighting

No cues

SCENE 5

To open: Overall outdoor lighting

No cues

SCENE 6

To open: Overall indoor lighting

No cues

EFFECTS PLOT

Cue 13   **Frank** enters   (Page 95)
               "She Loves You" plays until the end of scene

Cue 14   **Morley** lies listening   (Page 96)
               Sound of car starting up

Cue 15   **Robert** enters   (Page 96)
               Sound of car driving off